My CBT Journal

A CBT WORKBOOK TO HELP YOU RECORD YOUR PROGRESS USING CBT

Written by Dr James Manning &
Dr Nicola Ridgeway

Published by The West Suffolk CBT Service
Angel Corner
8 Angel Hill
Bury St Edmunds
Suffolk
England

Elige Cogniscere

My CBT journal: A CBT workbook and diary to help you record your progress using CBT. This workbook is full of blank CBT worksheets, tables and diagrams that can be used to accompany CBT therapy and CBT books.

Written by

Dr James Manning, ClinPsyD
Dr Nicola Ridgeway, ClinPsyD

Published by

The West Suffolk CBT Service Ltd, Angel Corner, 8 Angel Hill, Bury St Edmunds, Suffolk, IP33 1UZ

About the authors

Dr Nicola Ridgeway is a Consultant Clinical Psychologist and an accredited cognitive and behavioural therapist. She lectured on cognitive behaviour therapy (CBT) at the University of East Anglia, Suffolk, England, and the University of Essex for many years before becoming the Clinical Director of the West Suffolk CBT Service Ltd. Together with Dr James Manning she has co-authored several books on CBT.

Dr James Manning is a Consultant Clinical Psychologist and the Managing Director of the West Suffolk CBT Service. James has post-graduate qualifications in both Clinical Psychology and Counselling Psychology. He has regularly offered workshops and training to clinicians throughout the United Kingdom on Cognitive Behaviour Therapy and continues to work as a practicing therapist.

By the authors

Think About Your Thinking to Stop Depression

How to Help Your Loved One Overcome Depression

CBT for Panic Attacks

The Little Book on CBT for Depression

Cognitive Behaviour Therapy for Social Anxiety and Shyness

A Simple Introduction to Cognitive Behaviour Therapy for Visual Learners

CBT Worksheets

CBT: What it is and how it works (2nd Edition)

My CBT Journal

CBT Worksheets for Anxiety

A Journey with Panic

CBT Worksheets for Teenage Social Anxiety

Breaking free from social anxiety

Fused: A memoir of childhood OCD and adult obsession

How to befriend, tame, manage and teach your black dog called depression using CBT

Contents

Preface

by Dr James Manning

I suffered with mental health problems for many years before I got the help I needed, and in more stressful periods of my life, I experienced panic attacks from time-to-time. Fortunately, I found a way through my panic attacks by reading self-help books. Perhaps reading such books stimulated my interest in psychology, it's hard to say for sure. One thing I am grateful for is the freedom that psychological knowledge has given me. It has given me a life I value living and it has offered me an opportunity to help many others along the way.

At the risk of sounding a total f**k-up I'll tell you a bit about my life. Hopefully, it will give you some kind of an idea about how I developed such a passionate interest in psychology.

I have always had quite an obsessive personality and in my early teenage years I had quite a few problems with obsessive compulsive disorder. I knew that I was different from other people at a very young age, as did my family, but I didn't have any explanation for it. As I got older, I attempted to cope with problems that life presented me using food, drugs, gambling, and alcohol. I developed a significant alcohol problem as soon as I looked old enough to buy alcohol from an off-licence, (which was when I was about 17).

Between the ages of 15 and 30, I experienced a type of depression, known as dysthymia. Before this, I experienced sensory hyper-sensitivity, excessive avoidance, attention deficit, significant obsessive problems, paranoia, and anxiety.

In my late teenage years the emotion that affected me the most was low mood – I had a feeling of being slowed down, and an emptiness that sapped my motivation to engage in life. Normal events seemed more effortful and I found myself withdrawing from day-to-day activities. I started to feel unsettled most of the time, waking up early for no apparent reason – often at 4 am – churning thoughts over and over in my mind, and not being able to go back to sleep. I withdrew from people, preferring to be alone. I became snappy and irritable, and felt on edge. My relationships generally suffered, and I lost most of my friendships.

I didn't have a very eventful childhood, relatively speaking, at least not when compared to stories I have heard from many of my clients. I was bullied physically by older children and bullied emotionally by my peers (mainly for being socially backward), and I experienced some backward), and I experienced some mild trauma. Both of my parents were working class people who performed well in their careers and rose through the ranks of their respective companies, in my father's case to a top management position. My father was a perfectionist and highly obsessive. His perfectionist nature paid huge dividends for him at work – financially and professionally. He supervised award winning civil engineering work. I saw an old photograph of him recently, being given an award by the Queen of England. He had a tendency to be obsessive in all areas, including at home, and became angry at even slight violations of his high standards. Let's say as a hormonal teenager, I violated his standards pretty much all of the time and he struggled with parenting me as a teenager. In retrospect, he probably found me quite difficult to parent because he noticed things in me that he didn't like about himself.

Both my parents emigrated from Ireland when they were teenagers. They were very young when thrust into the responsibilities of parenthood and as you might expect from young parents, they didn't really have much experience of looking after children, but they were really no different from my friends' parents. I think my parents did their best to bring me up, based on the knowledge they had, but I struggled with being a child. I can still hear my mother's voice saying the words she repeated almost daily in her soft Irish accent: 'Childhood are the best years of your life, enjoy it while you can.' This confused me as my childhood felt terrible! And, and to make matters worse it seemed like my life was going to go downhill even further if these were the best years of my life. I had low self-esteem, and deeply entrenched beliefs that I was inadequate, stupid, bad, defective, weak, weird, and worthless as a person. I had no one I could talk to so I kept my fears to myself and spent a a lot of my time fighting my beliefs, keeping them hidden while I worked to prove them wrong.

As a young person, there were a number of positives that I could have drawn something from. By the time I reached 15, outsiders would have considered me a privileged child. I had some friends, and I had the support of a well-off family. I lived in a leafy suburb just outside London, and I had gained entry to a state selective grammar school, which at the time was one of the top schools in the country.

Unfortunately, however, I was not able to use what I had been given. By the age of 15, depression had started to hit me quite hard and my motivation to engage in life began to drop significantly. School teachers were not impressed with my academic performance and reported back to my parents that I was under-achieving academically. I passed my first set of exams at 16 and went on to do advanced exams, where I achieved less than spectacular results. By the time I was doing my advanced exams, teachers had noticed the changes in my behaviour and had begun to monitor me more closely. One day my chemistry teacher approached me with a frown etched on his forehead – even more than usual – and muttered, 'If you're not paranoid you should be!' A short time later I was told that the teachers held a meeting about me and I was placed on report; this is where teachers monitor a student much more closely and have regular meetings with them. By then I had dropped out of most of my sports teams such as rugby and cross-country, I struggled with my friendship groups and eventually found myself dropped from them.

Things weren't really going too well from a teenager's point of view. By this time, I already felt that I was a failure in life.

After leaving school you could say that I had a lucky break and gained a position in a small commodity brokers. I struggled to retain this role, not because of my ability to do the technical part of the job, but because of my lack of ability to regulate my mood and deal with interpersonal conflict. Basically, I found it difficult to get on with people. One day I found myself challenging a commodity trader for breaking what I thought were the rules of trading. The problem was that he worked for a very important client. The next day I was invited to my Managing Director's office and given my notice.

A number of further jobs followed, assisted at times by the support of my parents, but again I experienced interpersonal problems and had further dismissals. As time progressed, I found that my CV was beginning to look less and less promising as I moved from one job to another. On paper I thought I had begun to look unemployable and out of desperation began working for financial companies with dubious or unethical outlooks. I took a job in London working for a company that I hadn't looked into too much. I soon discovered after reading letters from clients that the company had previously been a very sophisticated boiler house. I couldn't work for companies like this, due to my moral stance on life. Following this, I continued to work my way down the pay scale hierarchy. Eventually the only work I could find was temporary work in factories, delivering pizza, and working as a cleaner for a minimum wage. A friend of mine Jo, a fund manager at Hill Samuel (a leading Merchant bank in London at the time) tried to call me and left messages with my parents over a period of several months. I didn't return his calls. I treated him very poorly considering we had developed a close friendship over a number of years. I basically abandoned him with no thought about how it might affect him.

Moving from plush offices to factories and such was a bit of a culture shock for me and I was dismissed from two of my minimum wage cleaning jobs for not following the requested instructions. I am embarrassed to admit that practically the only job I didn't get the sack from before I was 28 was my pizza delivery job at Pizza Hut, and even that job was painful sometimes. From time-to-time I found myself delivering pizza to some of my now successful Grammar School peers who appeared speechless when they opened their door to find me standing there with a pizza for them.

By that time my sense of inadequacy was fully reinforced and I had switched off emotionally. During this period of time I became quite hard-up financially and my mind set had become quite extreme and rigid. I didn't want to use the unemployment system or to ask my parents for help as in my mind this would have confirmed to me that I really was not succeeding in life. Sometimes I couldn't earn enough money to pay rent, so I ended up spending months living in a tent at a campsite where the rent was £4 per day. At other At other times I could pay the rent but was left eating potatoes and baked beans as my only source of nourishment. I continuously felt that

I was failing in some way. I felt empty inside. I just didn't feel like I had the energy to do things; I wanted to escape from my problems and myself. The only time I really felt OK was when I was asleep. I became quite avoidant and more nocturnal. I often did not attend events that I had been invited to, mostly without sending an apology or letting people know. I didn't answer the phone to friends or return their calls. The number of friends I had dwindled to just one. I think the only way that this friend managed to tolerate me was to laugh about the way I behaved, and to recognise that my behaviour was not about him. I felt so insignificant that I genuinely believed other people wouldn't notice or care whether I turned up late for planned events, or would even be bothered if I attended them at all. *All my focus was on myself.* It was a pitiful kind of self-loathing with endless self-questioning about why my life was so broken. I was so detached that I had little regard for other people's feelings or my own. Most of the time I did not want to live anymore and hoped I would die.* It was as if my body, mind, and my personality, were so unacceptable to me that I despised myself.

Luckily, in my very late twenties and early thirties I found a few excellent therapists. I worked hard on my therapy – which in my case needed a couple of years, as I had left things for so long before getting help. I brought negative and self-defeating thoughts that I had into conscious awareness and began to make significant changes to my life. I changed my life using many of the processes I have covered in this book. I'm 49 now, and I have been fortunate to have worked with Dr Nicola Ridgeway in treating several thousand clients over the years, and I haven't looked back since. I am still grateful to have the opportunity to help others who are stuck to move on with their lives.

I continue to use many of the exercises and coping strategies that I learnt in my therapy to keep in a good state of well-being. I can state categorically that if I were to stop using my coping strategies now, I would very quickly drift back into mental health problems. I have learnt that Cognitive Behaviour Therapy (CBT) is not a quick fix. Many people make initial positive gains after a completing a course of CBT, but most relapse after a number of years. This does not mean that CBT is not effective, as it works when people are using it. In reality, it means that people have stopped using the strategies that they worked on during their therapy. An important message that I would like to get across to you, therefore, is that CBT is delivered over a short time, <u>but it is not a short-term therapy</u>

---

*Except when I had panic attacks. I really didn't want to die when I had those.

How to use this book

I wrote this book because I found that many of my clients found it very difficult to remember topics discussed in their CBT sessions. I discovered that giving people hand-outs tended to help a bit, but that sheets of A4 paper tended to get lost quite easily. I wanted to find a way to help my clients to keep a permanent record of their progress, so that they could look back over what they did at any time in the future. The outcome is the book that you are reading right now.

Making records can be very helpful when completing CBT. You can write notes in this book before, during, and after your sessions. This book can be used as a memory aid, and to complete homework tasks set by your therapist.

Many people don't like writing in books, and in most of the CBT books I've looked at the pages are a little too small to write in. So I've made this book especially large, just so you can write in it. So please write in it! Write all over it if you like. If you are having one-to-one CBT sessions take it with you to your sessions, and use it to make notes during, or after your sessions.

When you have CBT, your therapist might not always have the worksheets that you need, and sometimes the sheets that are given out can end up all over the place. This book will help you to keep your sheets in one place, so that they don't get misplaced or lost. You can also use this book to complete homework tasks set by yourself and your therapist in sessions.

Chapter 1
Why use a journal?

Good CBT is based on accurate information collection. Your therapist will collect information from you during the time of your assessment, or as therapy progresses. You can also supply additional valuable information to your therapist through the use of diaries and CBT worksheets.

Diaries can be thought of as an inconvenience by many people, and sometimes it can be difficult to find the time to fill them in on a regular basis. I would really like to sell you the idea of using diaries, because they have multiple uses. They can assist you to a) observe yourself in a non-biased way and b) bring problems to therapy that you might otherwise forget to mention. Diaries also discourage the practice of 'screening out' or 'filtering out' relevant information through **selective attention**. Selective attention is where you see only what you want to see or decide what to see. This can happen consciously or **unconsciously** – by unconscious I mean processes that occur outside of your awareness.

A further hidden benefit of diaries is that they assist the practice of self-observation. Self-observation in written form puts less stress on the **pre-frontal cortex**, which as your therapist may discuss with you can become seriously affected in people with mental health problems, (Frodl et al, 2008). The pre-frontal cortex is a part of the brain that helps us to manage our emotions. We use the pre-frontal cortex to make choices, and to think about our thinking. It acts as a messenger between the higher analytical brain regions and lower brain regions – where emotions spring from. Finally, the pre-frontal cortex is used to quieten down 'noise' in the mind, and when it doesn't work so well we can find ourselves worrying about things that never used to bother us before.

Increased self-observation through the use of diaries also expands **working memory capacity**, which is beneficial to those individuals who are experiencing concentration difficulties as a result of anxiety and/or

Working memory is your ability to hold information in your mind and to think about it at the same time. You use your working memory to do things like mental arithmetic and to think about your thoughts.

In this book I have included several different types of diaries that you may or may not asked to use as part of your CBT therapy. There are thought, feeling, and behaviour diaries, as well as diaries that include a visual outline of the human body. Visually based diaries can be helpful to you, if you would like to draw where you notice your feelings most. Your therapist will show you how to complete part of a diary if he or she thinks that it is relevant for you to complete a diary as part of your homework.

Thought, feeling, physiology, and behaviour diaries

The diaries that are used most commonly in CBT are thought, physiology, feeling, and behaviour diaries – more generally known as 'thought records'. Thought records encourage the use of regular **body scanning -** which will be beneficial to you, as body scanning a) encourages you to notice what is happening in your body, thus encouraging greater sensory awareness and b) increases **experiential processing**. Experiential processing occurs when you learn through your senses and feelings, rather than when you learn through thinking or reading.

When I use the term **physiological reactions,** what I really mean is specific bodily changes that occur in the body. Specific body changes that you may notice when you are upset could be increased tension, jaw tightening, tight chest, pounding head, heart racing, heavy feelings in the legs, and such like. When I use the word **emotion**, I mean how you label and give meaning to specific bodily changes. Many physiological reactions connected to emotions are very similar, for example, the physiological changes associated with anxiety and anger both involve a) heart rate increase, b) a rise on blood pressure, c) tension in major muscle groups, and such like. However, similar bodily reactions can be perceived very differently, and result in different behavioural reactions. This is why I attach importance to the labelling of emotions.

Chapter 2
Problem lists

It will be useful to make a list of problems that you are experiencing at the earliest stage possible. Often it may not be possible to work with every problem on your list. However, a list will provide an opportunity for you to decide which problems are causing you the most distress.

When money for therapy is limited, or the number of sessions is fixed by an insurance company or by a government organisation, focussing on one specific area or working on just one problem at a time will help you to manage the therapeutic time you are offered more effectively. You can always return to therapy at a later stage to work on other problems.

A problem list is something that you can come back to at regular intervals to assess your progress. Going back to your problem list on a regular basis will also help you to identify how much forward movement you have made.

Therapy preparation sheet

Once you have a problem list, using a therapy preparation sheet can help you to narrow your focus further onto the problems you have selected, making your CBT even more manageable.

What goes on a problem-list?

Many of us are very good at identifying what doesn't feel right in our lives, and being as specific as possible about what your problems are will be very useful when it actually comes to completing CBT.

A good place to start a problem-list is to notice what things in your life make you feel emotionally distressed. Most people who come to CBT experience problems with anxiety, worry, panic attacks, depression, and anger. Feelings, however, are not the cause of your problem, they are a symptom of your problem. When you complete your problem list, it will be useful to have a think about what factors in your life are triggering your distressing emotions.

Examples of problems could include

- Asserting yourself in your relationships
- Having low self-esteem
- Difficulties managing workload
- Neglecting yourself through the use of certain behaviours, drugs, food, or alcohol
- Avoiding activities, behaviours or certain types of interactions
- Experiencing difficulties in how you react to your thoughts and feelings
- Expressing your feelings
- Difficulties dealing with confrontation
- Difficulties interacting the way that you want to with others
- Feeling disconnected from others
- Carrying out unhelpful behaviours that stop you progressing in life
- Reacting negatively to yourself
- Feeling hijacked by your emotions
- Unresolved painful experiences from your past that still affect you in the present

Therapy preparation sheet

A therapy preparation sheet will help you to focus your mind on the problem that you are working on. Acknowledging that you have a problem is the first step that you will need to make in creating change. Working through the details of a problem can be very useful as it can bring to mind the small things that tend to keep your problem in place. Later on, these details will help you to resolve the problem. An example of a therapy preparation sheet has been completed at the end of this chapter, and I have left some blank worksheets for you to complete by yourself.

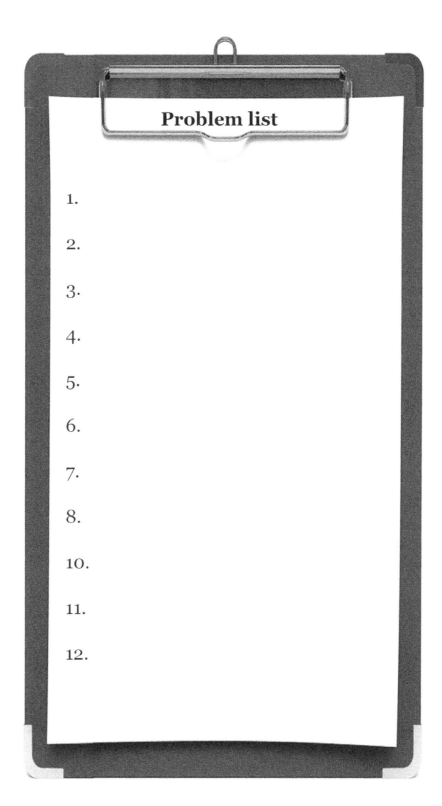

Problem list

1.

2.

3.

4.

5.

6.

7.

8.

10.

11.

12.

Therapy preparation sheet

Describe the problem that I have been experiencing

I keep arguing with my partner in front of my children. The arguments are often over pointless little things and they make my children anxious and upset.

How long has this problem been around for?

This problem has been around for as long as I can remember. We both have a problem backing down.

What may have triggered this problem?

Being told that I have done something wrong is the main trigger, or being criticised.

How have I attempted to resolve my problem?

I try to keep the conversation short if I see an argument beginning, but my partner then starts to become anxious that I am being distant.

What are the main things that keep my problem in place?

Arguing back generally makes it worse. If I criticise my partner back it can end up in a war that seems to go on for days.

What will I need to do to resolve this problem?

Find a different way to reacting to my partner's comments. It takes two people to keep the argument going.

How would my life be different without this problem?

Life would be more peaceful and there would be less negative energy floating around the house. The children would feel more relaxed.

Therapy preparation sheet

Describe the problem that I have been experiencing

How long has this problem been around for?

What may have triggered this problem?

How have I attempted to resolve my problem?

What are the main things that keep my problem in place?

What will I need to do to resolve this problem?

How would my life be different without this problem?

Therapy preparation sheet

Describe the problem that I have been experiencing

How long has this problem been around for?

What may have triggered this problem?

How have I attempted to resolve my problem?

What are the main things that keep my problem in place?

What will I need to do to resolve this problem?

How would my life be different without this problem?

Chapter 3
Mood diaries

Mood diary

Mood diaries can be highly beneficial as they can help pinpoint triggers in your environment that may lead to you feeling an increase in distress. They can also be useful if you are depressed or if you have memory difficulties. Completing a mood diary can highlight changes in mood that occur during the day, and help you to monitor your mood over time. This information from your mood diary may also be useful to your psychiatrist or GP if you are receiving medication or if your medication is being reviewed.

Activity schedule

If you are having one-to-one CBT, there is a small chance that your therapist may ask you to complete an activity schedule. The activity schedule is a very powerful tool in CBT if it is used correctly, and it can act as a source of intervention and assessment. In most cases measures of enjoyment and achievement are recorded, although your therapist can pick other measures that he or she thinks are more relevant to you. As a tool the activity schedule encourages much greater reflection on activities that can contribute to an enjoyable life, and it can help you to identify how a rule-based existence (e.g., "If I get things done, then I will be OK) does not necessarily lead to an improvement in mood.

Other diaries

We have included a selection of other diaries in this chapter. These diaries can be utilised to focus on particular areas in need of development. With this in mind, we have included diaries to record the impact of intrusive thoughts, anger reactions and problematic behaviours. As with all diaries these thought, feeling and behaviour based records are designed to encourage you to increase distance from your problems and to look at things from a different perspective.

Mood diaries and activity schedules

Mood diaries are very useful for keeping track of your mood and becoming aware of what types of activity result in mood changes. Most of the time memory alone is unreliable when it comes to recalling what activities impact on our mood. Often the most valid way to assess your mood is to make a record while you are experiencing it. Depression in particular can result in fluctuations in mood throughout the day. There may also be aspects of your life or behaviours that you engage in that have a significant impact on your mood that you are not aware of. Keeping track of your mood will help you to identify external or internal aspects of your life that are keeping your emotional distress in place. If you notice fluctuations in your mood this is also a potential area for discussion with your therapist or with your psychiatrist/GP if you are receiving medication.

Mood Diary

Please use this diary to keep a record of your mood. For each time period give yourself a score between 0 and 10 where 10 is the most that you can experience a feeling.

For the positive feeling box please rate how positive you felt during each time period as a whole. Examples of positivity may include being interested, excited, enthusiastic, strong, proud etc.

For the negative feeling box please rate how negative you felt during the time period. Examples of negativity may include feeling distressed, hostile, afraid, upset, ashamed and such like.

Day ___ Date ___

Time period	Positive feeling 0 to 10	Negative feeling 0 to 10
6am to 12pm		
12pm to 6pm		
6pm to 12am		

Day ___ Date ___

Time period	Positive feeling 0 to 10	Negative feeling 0 to 10
6am to 12pm		
12pm to 6pm		
6pm to 12am		

Day ___ Date ___

Time period	Positive feeling 0 to 10	Negative feeling 0 to 10
6am to 12pm		
12pm to 6pm		
6pm to 12am		

Day ___ Date ___

Time period	Positive feeling 0 to 10	Negative feeling 0 to 10
6am to 12pm		
12pm to 6pm		
6pm to 12am		

Day ___ Date ___

Time period	Positive feeling 0 to 10	Negative feeling 0 to 10
6am to 12pm		
12pm to 6pm		
6pm to 12am		

Day ___ Date ___

Time period	Positive feeling 0 to 10	Negative feeling 0 to 10
6am to 12pm		
12pm to 6pm		
6pm to 12am		

Day ___ Date ___

Time period	Positive feeling 0 to 10	Negative feeling 0 to 10
6am to 12pm		
12pm to 6pm		
6pm to 12am		

Day ___ Date ___

Time period	Positive feeling 0 to 10	Negative feeling 0 to 10
6am to 12pm		
12pm to 6pm		
6pm to 12am		

Day ___ Date ___

Time period	Positive feeling 0 to 10	Negative feeling 0 to 10
6am to 12pm		
12pm to 6pm		
6pm to 12am		

Mood Diary

Please use this diary to keep a record of your mood. For each time period give yourself a score between 0 and 10 where 10 is the most that you can experience a feeling.

For the positive feeling box please rate how positive you felt during each time period as a whole. Examples of positivity may include being interested, excited, enthusiastic, strong, proud etc.

For the negative feeling box please rate how negative you felt during the time period. Examples of negativity may include feeling distressed, hostile, afraid, upset, ashamed and such like.

Day / **Date**

Time period	Positive feeling 0 to 10	Negative feeling 0 to 10
6am to 12pm		
12pm to 6pm		
6pm to 12am		

Day / **Date**

Time period	Positive feeling 0 to 10	Negative feeling 0 to 10
6am to 12pm		
12pm to 6pm		
6pm to 12am		

Day / **Date**

Time period	Positive feeling 0 to 10	Negative feeling 0 to 10
6am to 12pm		
12pm to 6pm		
6pm to 12am		

Day / **Date**

Time period	Positive feeling 0 to 10	Negative feeling 0 to 10
6am to 12pm		
12pm to 6pm		
6pm to 12am		

Day / **Date**

Time period	Positive feeling 0 to 10	Negative feeling 0 to 10
6am to 12pm		
12pm to 6pm		
6pm to 12am		

Day / **Date**

Time period	Positive feeling 0 to 10	Negative feeling 0 to 10
6am to 12pm		
12pm to 6pm		
6pm to 12am		

Day / **Date**

Time period	Positive feeling 0 to 10	Negative feeling 0 to 10
6am to 12pm		
12pm to 6pm		
6pm to 12am		

Day / **Date**

Time period	Positive feeling 0 to 10	Negative feeling 0 to 10
6am to 12pm		
12pm to 6pm		
6pm to 12am		

Day / **Date**

Time period	Positive feeling 0 to 10	Negative feeling 0 to 10
6am to 12pm		
12pm to 6pm		
6pm to 12am		

Activity schedule

Write down the main thing that you are doing in each hour time period.

After you have completed the activity score yourself in terms of achievement and happiness giving yourself a score between 0 and 10, where 10 is the highest it can possibly be and 0 is the lowest.

H- Happiness
A- Achievement

Time	Monday Activity		Tuesday Activity		Wednesday Activity		Thursday Activity		Friday Activity		Saturday Activity		Sunday Activity	
8am to 9am		H		H		H		H		H		H		H
		A		A		A		A		A		A		A
9am to 10am		H		H		H		H		H		H		H
		A		A		A		A		A		A		A
10am to 11am		H		H		H		H		H		H		H
		A		A		A		A		A		A		A
11am to 12pm		H		H		H		H		H		H		H
		A		A		A		A		A		A		A
12m to 1pm		H		H		H		H		H		H		H
		A		A		A		A		A		A		A
1pm to 2pm		H		H		H		H		H		H		H
		A		A		A		A		A		A		A
2pm to 3pm		H		H		H		H		H		H		H
		A		A		A		A		A		A		A
3pm to 4pm		H		H		H		H		H		H		H
		A		A		A		A		A		A		A
4pm to 5pm		H		H		H		H		H		H		H
		A		A		A		A		A		A		A
5pm to 6pm		H		H		H		H		H		H		H
		A		A		A		A		A		A		A
6pm to 7pm		H		H		H		H		H		H		H
		A		A		A		A		A		A		A
7pm to 8pm		H		H		H		H		H		H		H
		A		A		A		A		A		A		A
8pm to 9pm		H		H		H		H		H		H		H
		A		A		A		A		A		A		A

Activity schedule

Write down the main thing that you are doing in each hour time period.

After you have completed the activity score yourself in terms of achievement and happiness giving yourself a score between 0 and 10, where 10 is the highest it can possibly be and 0 is the lowest.

H- Happiness
A- Achievement

Time	Activity		Activity		Activity		Activity		Activity		Activity		Activity	
	H	A	H	A	H	A	H	A	H	A	H	A	H	A
	H	A	H	A	H	A	H	A	H	A	H	A	H	A
	H	A	H	A	H	A	H	A	H	A	H	A	H	A
	H	A	H	A	H	A	H	A	H	A	H	A	H	A
	H	A	H	A	H	A	H	A	H	A	H	A	H	A
	H	A	H	A	H	A	H	A	H	A	H	A	H	A
	H	A	H	A	H	A	H	A	H	A	H	A	H	A
	H	A	H	A	H	A	H	A	H	A	H	A	H	A
	H	A	H	A	H	A	H	A	H	A	H	A	H	A
	H	A	H	A	H	A	H	A	H	A	H	A	H	A
	H	A	H	A	H	A	H	A	H	A	H	A	H	A

Activity schedule

Write down the main thing that you are doing in each hour time period.

Time	Activity	Activity	Activity	Activity	Activity	Activity	Activity

Daily activity diary

Time	Activity	Enjoyment 0 to 10	Attainment 0 to 10

Thoughts, feelings & behaviour diary			
Time: Date: Trigger situation:	Thoughts, e.g. "They must think that I'm an idiot?"	Emotion, e.g. anxiety, anger, shame, disgust	Behaviour, e.g. avoid a situation

Chapter 4
Thought diaries

Thought diaries can be used to focus on particular areas of your life that you would like to develop. In this chapter, I have included thought diaries to record the impact of intrusive thoughts, anger reactions, and problematic behaviours. All of these diaries are thought, feeling, and behaviour-based records. They are designed to encourage you to increase distance from your problems, and to look at things from a different viewpoint.

Thought, feeling, physiology, and behaviour diaries

Once a problem has been identified the completion of thought, feeling, and behaviour diaries can be extremely useful. Filling in these types of diaries will not only provide useful material that you can work on in sessions, but the process will also act as a low-level CBT exercise. Generally, most of us live our lives automatically, without giving much thought to a) thinking about our thinking, b) how we react to our feelings, or c) what makes us behave the way that we do.

Completing a diary brings more of our automatic processes into awareness. Once thinking patterns are brought into our conscious awareness, we immediately have more choice about how to react. This is due to the fact that writing information down about the self encourages a process of stepping back and observing. This will automatically encourage the use of self-reflection. As soon as we start to consider what makes us think, feel, or behave the way that we do, we engage the pre-frontal cortex*, which can often start to switch off when we become distressed.

Intrusive thoughts diary

Intrusive thoughts as their name suggests pop into the mind without crashes, planes exploding, being seriously ill, someone close to us dying, and such like. The majority of us dismiss these thoughts for what they are, just thoughts. Some people, however, can struggle with experiencing intrusive thoughts, thinking that because they have had these thoughts that a) something bad is going to happen and/or b) there is something wrong with them for having such thoughts. People who tend to struggle the most with intrusive thoughts are individuals who are prone to obsessive compulsive disorder (OCD). Many people with OCD engage in rituals or **neutralising behaviours** to reduce the emotional intensity of their thoughts. A neutralising behaviour is a behaviour that an individual completes in order to reduce or remove a feeling, for example, washing hands, placing things in a particular order, etc. An example of an intrusive thought diary is shown at the end of this chapter.

Anger diaries

Although for the most part, anger is a healthy, adaptive emotion, at times behaviour resulting from anger can have negative outcomes. If this is the case, then it will be useful to compete anger diaries. Completing an anger diary brings awareness to the types of thoughts that result in anger, and the consequences of angry behaviour. Increased mindfulness of our anger reactions can result in us making a choice to behave differently. It can be very difficult to complete an anger diary while feeling angry. If this is the case, complete your anger diary after your anger has faded away, or while your anger is decreasing.

Thoughts, feelings & behaviour diary

Time: Date: Trigger situation	Thoughts, e.g., 'They must think that I'm an idiot'	Emotion, e.g., anxiety, anger, shame, disgust	Behaviour, e.g., avoid situation
12.00pm 6 June Disagreement with an opposing football coach.	'He's going along with the referee's decision because it's easier for him. My reaction shows that there is something wrong with me. He's laughing at me and thinks I'm an idiot.'	Anxiety, anger, guilt, shame.	Raise a formal protest. Think of some different ways in which I can get him back. Churn the situation over in my mind for a couple of days. Feel guilty and ashamed about the way that I am thinking.

Intrusive thoughts diary

Time: Date: Trigger situation	Thoughts, e.g., an image of the self hurting someone.	Interpretation of thought, e.g., 'This means that I want to do it!'	Behaviour, e.g., avoid being alone with that person.
3 pm 29 March At work. Wondering what my son was up to at home.	Vivid image of my son when he is older hurting himself deliberately.	This is going to happen. I am a bad parent and it is my fault.	Become over-protective towards son. Do things for him.

Anger diary

Time: Date:	Trigger	Thoughts	Emotion	Bodily changes	Behaviour	Consequences of behaviour
8pm 4th May	In a team game an opponent making me look silly with his skilful play.	'He's making me look like an idiot.'	Frustration, anger with self.	Feeling hot, tense in the chest and arms.	Without thinking boot the ball up the pitch as the player is walking back after scoring.	The ball flies past the player's ear narrowly missing his head. To others watching it looks like I've tried to kick the ball at him on purpose.

Thoughts, feelings & behaviour diary

Time: Date: Trigger situation	Thoughts, e.g., 'They must think that I'm an idiot'	Emotion, e.g., anxiety, anger, shame, disgust	Behaviour, e.g., avoid situation

Thoughts, feelings & behaviour diary

Time: Date: Trigger situation	Thoughts, e.g., 'They must think that I'm an idiot'	Emotion, e.g., anxiety, anger, shame, disgust	Behaviour, e.g., avoid situation

Thoughts, feelings & behaviour diary

Time: Date: Trigger situation	Thoughts, e.g., 'They must think that I'm an idiot'	Emotion, e.g., anxiety, anger, shame, disgust	Behaviour, e.g., avoid situation

Anger diary

Time: Date:	Trigger	Thoughts	Emotion	Bodily changes	Behaviour	Consequences of behaviour

Anger diary

Time: Date:	Trigger	Thoughts	Emotion	Bodily changes	Behaviour	Consequences of behaviour

Anger diary

Time: Date:	Trigger	Thoughts	Emotion	Bodily changes	Behaviour	Consequences of behaviour

Intrusive thoughts diary

Time: Date: Trigger situation	Thoughts, e.g., an image of the self hurting someone.	Interpretation of thought, e.g., 'This means that I want to do it?'	Behaviour, e.g., avoid being alone with that person.

Intrusive thoughts diary

Time: Date: Trigger situation	Thoughts, e.g., an image of the self hurting someone.	Interpretation of thought, e.g., 'This means that I want to do it!'	Behaviour, e.g., avoid being alone with that person.

Intrusive thoughts diary

Time: Date: Trigger situation	Thoughts, e.g., an image of the self hurting someone.	Interpretation of thought, e.g., 'This means that I want to do it!'	Behaviour, e.g., avoid being alone with that person.

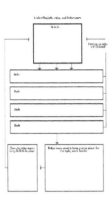

Chapter 5 Longitudinal formulations

A **longitudinal formulation** is one of the most important formulations* within CBT. A longitudinal formulation is a psychological explanation of how your problem has developed over time. Generally, it is drawn out by your therapist in an initial assessment, or early on in CBT sessions.

In this chapter I have included three of the most commonly used variations of longitudinal formulations. In each case, I have placed a completed example, followed by blank worksheets for you to fill in your own details.

A longitudinal formulation sets out clearly what makes you think, feel, and behave the way that you do. Longitudinal formulations usually contain information about your childhood experiences, beliefs, rules, and behaviours. Longitudinal formulations are cyclical in nature, and give you an indication of how your behaviour may have a tendency to reinforce your deepest fears over the passage of time.

Longitudinal CBT formulations usually include **limiting beliefs, rules, safety behaviours, negative automatic thoughts, and emotional responses**. I will explain what each of these is in order.

*A formulation is a psychological explanation of an individual's difficulties.

Beliefs

Longitudinal CBT formulations usually include **limiting beliefs**. In CBT literature, limiting beliefs are referred to as 'beliefs', 'core beliefs' or 'maladaptive beliefs'. Limiting beliefs are very strongly held negative ideas connected to the self and/or others and tend to be learnt as children. Limiting beliefs often have specific themes and fall into four general domains. These domains are: responsibility (e.g., 'I am bad'); self-defectiveness (e.g., 'I am flawed'); power and control (e.g., 'I am weak'); and safety (e.g., 'I am not safe', 'Others cannot be trusted'). Limiting beliefs have the capacity to hold back self-growth and because of this are often identified early on in cognitive behaviour therapy.

Within CBT, beliefs are regarded as unconditional and inflexible. You are likely to hold a limiting belief if you experience a strong emotional reaction that is more intense than most people might expect for any given situation. Beliefs operate at a felt level (experiential level) rather than a logical level. Beliefs can feel factual no matter how much evidence you have to the contrary. For example, many people who believe they are bad, may not have done anything seriously wrong in their lives and may spend a lot of time thinking or caring about how others feel (which, of course, is an unusual characteristic for people who really are bad). Beliefs have a tendency to retain their perceived experiential validity (i.e., they still feel true) whatever you think, do or say and can be triggered over and over again with the same results. Beliefs are very difficult to challenge in CBT as they carry an intense emotional charge, and are often held with strong conviction (or in other words, we tend to believe them very strongly). Luckily, the rigidity and validity of beliefs can be loosened through the use of specific CBT experiential exercises that focus on challenging the 'believability' of beliefs.

Rules and conditional assumptions

Rules and conditional assumptions are ideas that we put in place knowingly or unknowingly to protect ourselves from our limiting beliefs. Unlike beliefs, which are unconditional (which means they are there whatever you think, feel say or do), rules are **conditional**. Conditional means that if you or others meet certain conditions then your rules can be met and you can decide that you are OK. Rules often trigger bargaining within the self and you may find yourself changing your behaviour to keep your rules intact or to accommodate your rules. An alternative method that people use to keep their rules intact is to avoid situations that challenge their rules. For example, if you hold a rule 'If I am successful at all times then I will be OK' you could try harder to make sure that you are successful or alternatively you may completely avoid putting yourself in challenging situations, (where you might not be successful). Other examples of rules include, 'If I am strong and in control at all times, then I will be OK' or 'If others are happy with me and I say 'yes' to requests at all times, then I will be OK'; 'If I appear normal then I will be OK' and 'If I appear competent at all times then I will be OK'. You can identify whether you have a rule by assessing whether you have a strong emotional reaction when you are unable, for whatever reason, to meet the conditions of your rule. Examining your emotional reactions to events is likely to be the main method that your CBT therapist will use to identify whether you have a rule in place.

Rules are slightly easier than beliefs to challenge using CBT. To challenge rules, you will need to learn adaptive coping strategies so that you can help regulate or soothe the strong emotions that are likely to arise as a result of not following your rules or breaking your rules. Rule violations can occur over extended periods of time – years in some cases. (A rule violation ostensibly means that a rule has been broken or is in the process of being broken.) The effect of rule violations may be low mood, depression and anxiety. Equally, rules can be broken for a short duration a few minutes – for example – with the most common emotions being anxiety, anger, guilt, shame, and disgust.

Avoidance and safety behaviours

The use of **avoidance and safety behaviours** (also known as **maladaptive coping strategies)** are common among people who experience psychological distress. If we are experiencing avoidance, we may recognise that this is occurring if we feel inclined to deliberately stay away from situations where we feel uncomfortable emotions. Alternatively, we may be using safety behaviours when we approach situations that create fear. Examples of coping strategies include, focusing on yourself, distracting yourself, avoiding conflict, saying 'Yes' to all requests, worrying about how you might cope, distracting yourself, planning escape routes and such like. If you are using avoidance and/or safety behaviours these are likely to keep your problems in place; and, as time progresses, continued use of them can lead to a gradual loss of self-esteem and self-confidence.

Negative automatic thoughts

Negative automatic thoughts or NATs are the types of thoughts that run in the back of our minds when we are distressed. NATs are particularly likely to be in operation if we are experiencing depression or anxiety. NATs are important to identify because they can have a big impact on the way that we feel. NATs (unlike beliefs) are relatively easy to challenge using CBT. They tend to be situation specific and very biased. They are narrow and simplistic in their content. Examples of NAT's may include: 'People will find me boring'; 'I've got nothing to offer; 'People always treat me like this.' NATs can often have different levels of feeling attached to them. Christine Padesky, author of the best-selling CBT book *Mind Over Mood* suggests that some of the best NATs to identify and work with are **'hot cognitions.'** Hot cognitions are basically NATs that carry high degrees of distressing emotion with them. Hot cognitions are generally connected to core beliefs at some level.

Example of a longitudinal CBT model adapted from Judith Beck. Beck J. (2011). *Cognitive therapy: Basics and beyond*; **The Guildford Press**

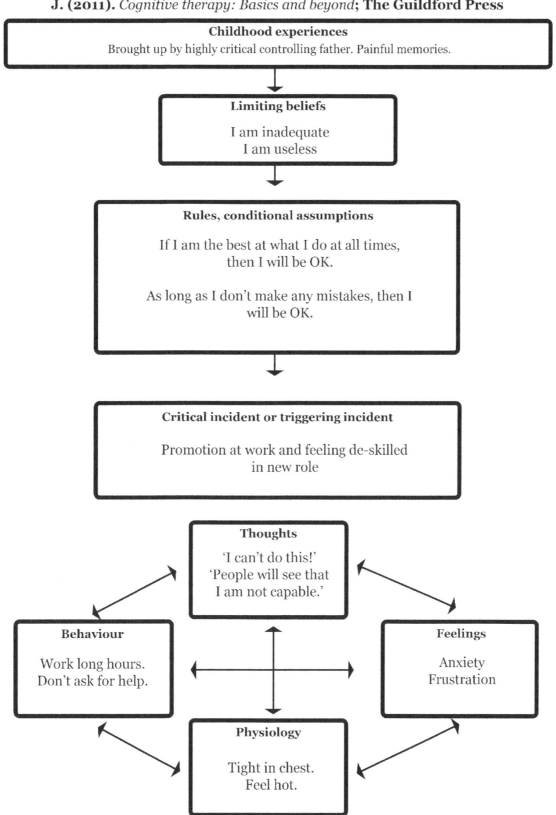

Childhood experiences
Brought up by highly critical controlling father. Painful memories.

Limiting beliefs

I am inadequate
I am useless

Rules, conditional assumptions

If I am the best at what I do at all times,
then I will be OK.

As long as I don't make any mistakes, then I
will be OK.

Critical incident or triggering incident

Promotion at work and feeling de-skilled
in new role

Thoughts
'I can't do this!'
'People will see that
I am not capable.'

Behaviour

Work long hours.
Don't ask for help.

Feelings

Anxiety
Frustration

Physiology

Tight in chest.
Feel hot.

Cycle of beliefs, rules and behaviours

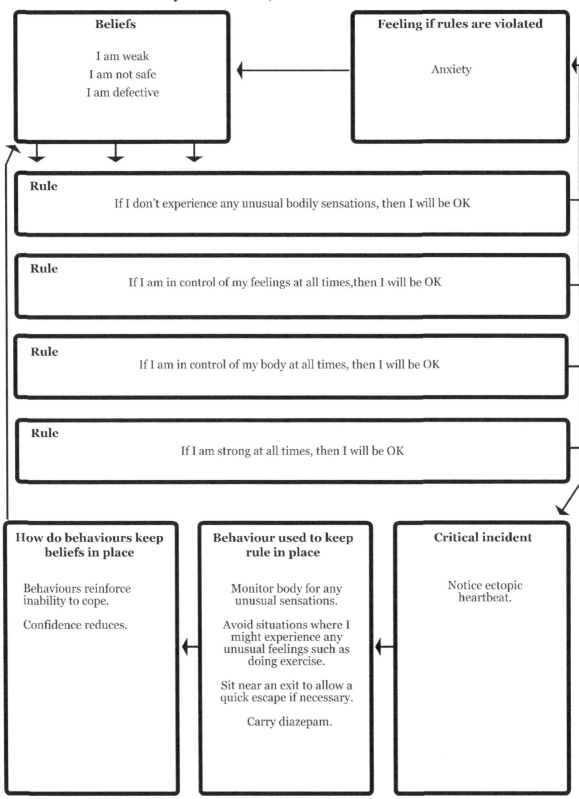

Beliefs

I am weak
I am not safe
I am defective

Feeling if rules are violated

Anxiety

Rule

If I don't experience any unusual bodily sensations, then I will be OK

Rule

If I am in control of my feelings at all times, then I will be OK

Rule

If I am in control of my body at all times, then I will be OK

Rule

If I am strong at all times, then I will be OK

How do behaviours keep beliefs in place

Behaviours reinforce inability to cope.

Confidence reduces.

Behaviour used to keep rule in place

Monitor body for any unusual sensations.

Avoid situations where I might experience any unusual feelings such as doing exercise.

Sit near an exit to allow a quick escape if necessary.

Carry diazepam.

Critical incident

Notice ectopic heartbeat.

Cycle of beliefs, rules and behaviours

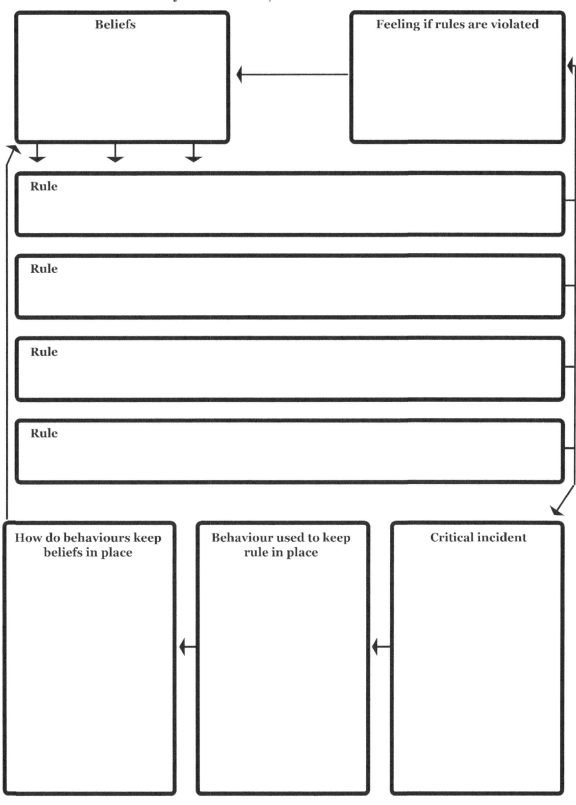

Beliefs

Feeling if rules are violated

Rule

Rule

Rule

Rule

How do behaviours keep beliefs in place

Behaviour used to keep rule in place

Critical incident

Rule sheet: Use the box to the right to note which rules apply to you	✔
If I am in control at all times, then I will be OK	
If people are happy with me at all times, then I will be OK	
If I do things perfectly at all times, then I will be OK	
If I am the best at what I do at all times, then I will be OK	
If I don't experience any any unusual bodily sensations, then I will be OK	
If I am feeling good at all times, then I will be OK	
If I am feeling confident at all times, then I will be OK	
If I am not blamed for things, then I will be OK	
If I show dominance at all times, then I will be OK	
If I perform well at all times, then I will be OK	
If I am physically well at all times, then I will be OK	
If I am assertive at all times, then I will be OK	
If I know what I am doing at all times, then I will be OK	
If I know what is going to happen at all times, then I will be OK	
If I appear to others as though I know what I am doing, then I will be OK	
If I feel safe at all times, then I will be OK	
If I appear competent at all times, then I will be OK	
If I show no signs of vulnerability, then I will be OK	
If I am in control of my feelings at all times, then I will be OK	
If I say 'Yes' to all requests at all times, then I will be OK	
If I am strong at all times, then I will be OK	
If things go wrong it is all my fault	
If I don't let people down, then I will be OK	
If I can fix things, then I will be OK	
If I am in control of my body at all times, then I will be OK	
Total number of rules endorsed (write total number of rules endorsed in right-hand column)	

From *How to befriend, tame, manage and teach your Black Dog called Depression using CBT* by Dr James Manning

Rule sheet: Use the box to the right to note which rules apply to you	✔
If others don't challenge me, then I will be OK	
If people are happy with me at all times, then I will be OK	
If people around me don't make any mistakes, then I will be OK	
If others tell me that I am the best at what I do at all times, then I will be OK	
If people around me are happy, calm and relaxed, then I will be OK	
If people around me are polite and respectful, then I will be OK	
If people around me are confident, then I will be OK	
If others don't criticise me, then I will be OK	
If others let me take charge, then I will be OK	
If people around me appreciate me, then I will be OK	
If people around tell me that I am alright, then I will be OK	
If people listen to me at all times, then I will be OK	
If people around me know what they are doing at all times, then I will be OK	
If others reassure me, then I will be OK	
If others show confidence in me at all times, then I will be OK	
If others help me feel safe, then I will be OK	
If others approve of me at all times, then I will be OK	
If others show no signs of vulnerability, then I will be OK	
If others put my needs ahead of their own, then I will be OK	
If others say "Yes" to my requests when I ask them, then I will be OK	
If I am around strong people, then I will be OK	
If others take the blame for mistakes, then I will be OK	
If others don't let me down, then I will be OK	
If others can fix things for me, then I will be OK	
If others are there for me when I need them, then I will be OK	
Total number of rules endorsed (write number of rules endorsed in right-hand column)	

From *How to befriend, tame, manage and teach your Black Dog called Depression using CBT* by Dr James Manning

Old cycle/new cycle

Past

Old beliefs

'I am incompetent'

'I am not likeable'

'I am insignificant'

Old rules

If I am in control of my environment at all times, then I will be OK.

If others like me at all times, then I will be OK.

If I am in control of my feelings at all times, then I will be OK.

If others notice my achievements at all times, then I will be OK.

Old behaviours

Keep feelings to self.

Check and double check everything.

Try to predict problems before they happen.

Keep problems to myself.

Say "Yes" to all requests.

Concentrate on getting everything correct.

Future

New beliefs

'I am OK'

'I am me'

'I am free'

New rules

It's normal to tell people how I feel.

It's OK to assert my needs.

It's important that I make room for my feelings.

It's OK to make mistakes as long as I learn from them.

New behaviours

Tell others how I feel.

Assert myself when I want to do something.

Share problems with trusted others.

Check things once or just a few times.

Validate and accept my feelings.

Be myself.

Old cycle/new cycle

Past	Future
Old beliefs	**New beliefs**
↓	↓
Old rules	**New rules**
↓	↓
Old behaviours	**New behaviours**

Chapter 6
CBT cycles

CBT maintenance cycles or maintenance formulations are psychological explanations that draw attention to what is happening in the present. Most maintenance cycles focus on thoughts, physiological reactions, feelings and behaviours that keep specific problems in place. The most commonly used maintenance cycle is the generic CBT model although there are now many variations connected to specific problems or disorders.

In this chapter we have included the generic CBT model, a standard thoughts, feelings behaviour cycle, a model of social anxiety, a CBT model for panic, obsessive compulsive disorder (OCD) models, and Manning and Ridgeway's self-phobic model. These models can be used with more than 95% of presenting problems.

The generic CBT model

Before completing a generic CBT model it is usually practical to have a completed thought diary ready, so that you have a range of negative automatic thoughts (NATs) to work with. A good starting point is to look through the thoughts in your diary and pick out the thought that produces the most distressing emotion.

Once you have selected a NAT, verbally repeat the NAT in your mind for a little while and then complete a **body scan.** A body scan will involve you bringing awareness to your body and noticing physiological changes and emotions that accompany the NAT. The meaning behind the NAT can be identified by asking yourself, 'If this thought were true, what would it say or mean about me?'

A generic CBT cycle can be very useful in bringing to mind how self-fulfilling prophecies work. A natural continuation after drawing out such a cycle is the completion of a NAT challenging exercise, which you are also likely to learn about in CBT. Following NAT challenging exercises, more balanced thoughts can be inserted into a positive CBT cycle, which hopefully will demonstrate to you how you can easily alternate between positive and negative self-fulfilling prophecies, each of which can be equally predictable. One cycle is likely to be painful and self-limiting, whereas the other cycle is likely to be productive.

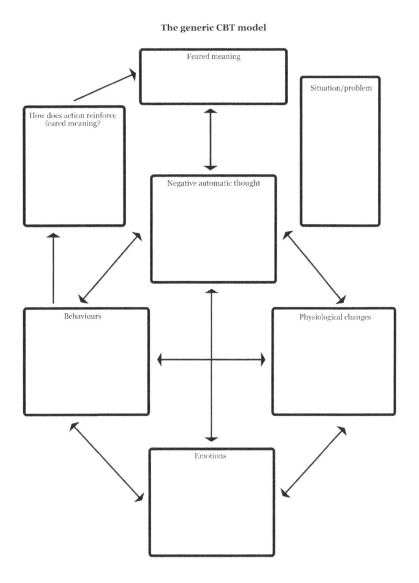

The generic CBT model

Feared meaning

Situation/problem

How does action reinforce feared meaning?

Negative automatic thought

Behaviours

Physiological changes

Emotions

The generic CBT model

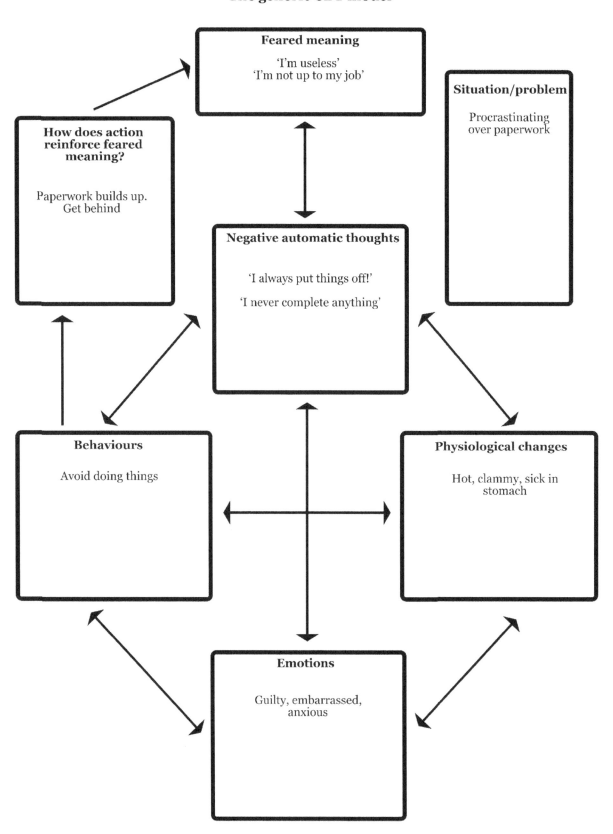

Feared meaning

'I'm useless'
'I'm not up to my job'

Situation/problem

Procrastinating
over paperwork

How does action reinforce feared meaning?

Paperwork builds up.
Get behind

Negative automatic thoughts

'I always put things off!'

'I never complete anything'

Behaviours

Avoid doing things

Physiological changes

Hot, clammy, sick in
stomach

Emotions

Guilty, embarrassed,
anxious

The generic CBT model

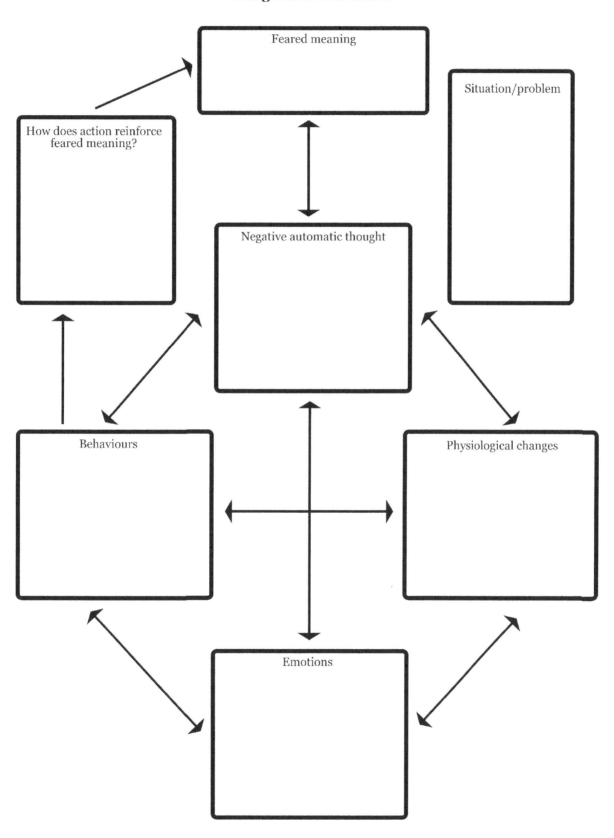

The generic CBT model

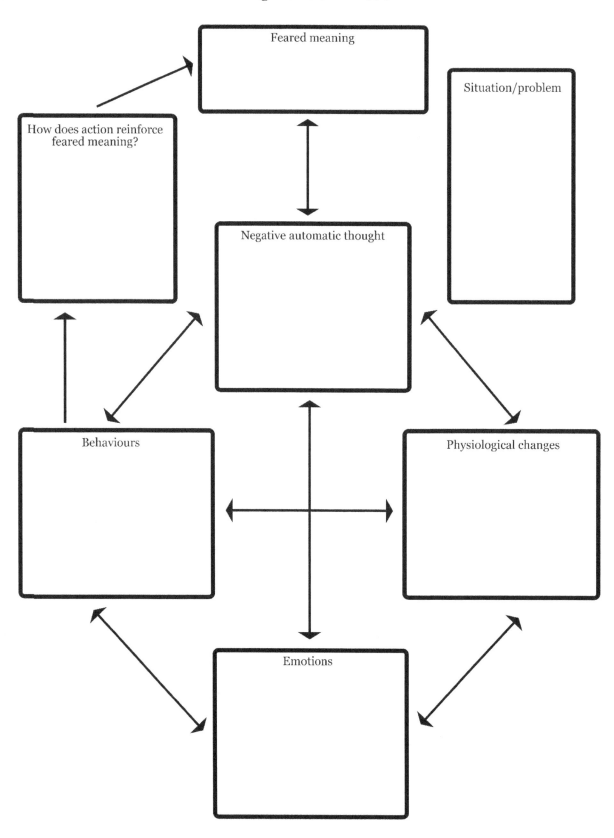

The generic CBT model

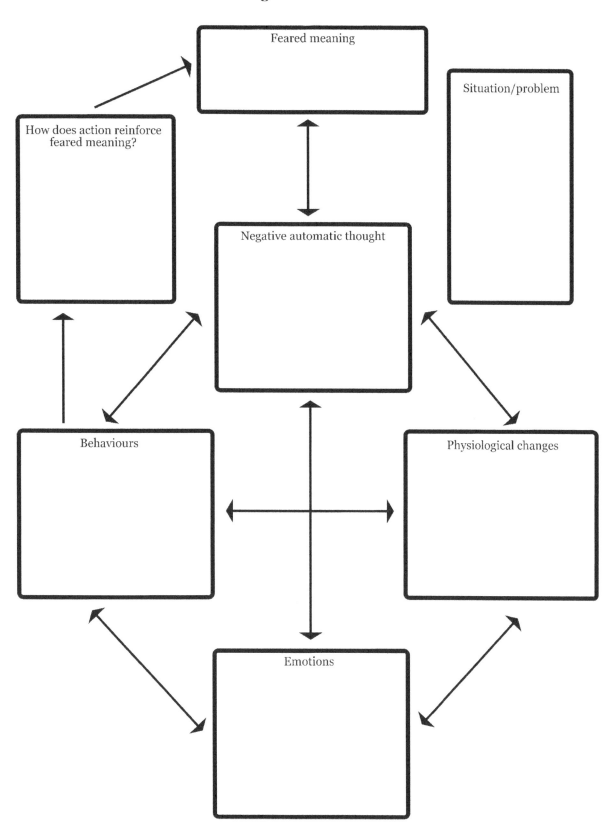

The generic CBT model

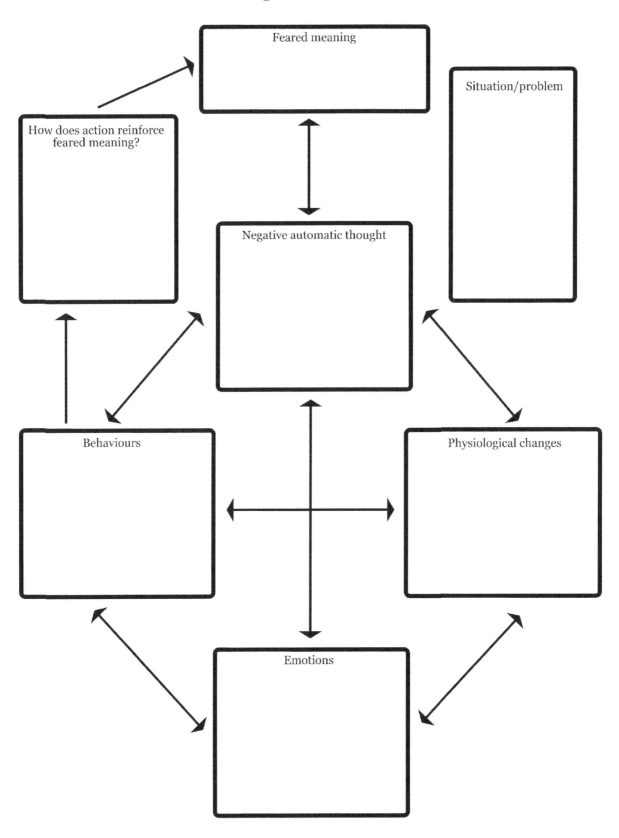

The generic CBT model

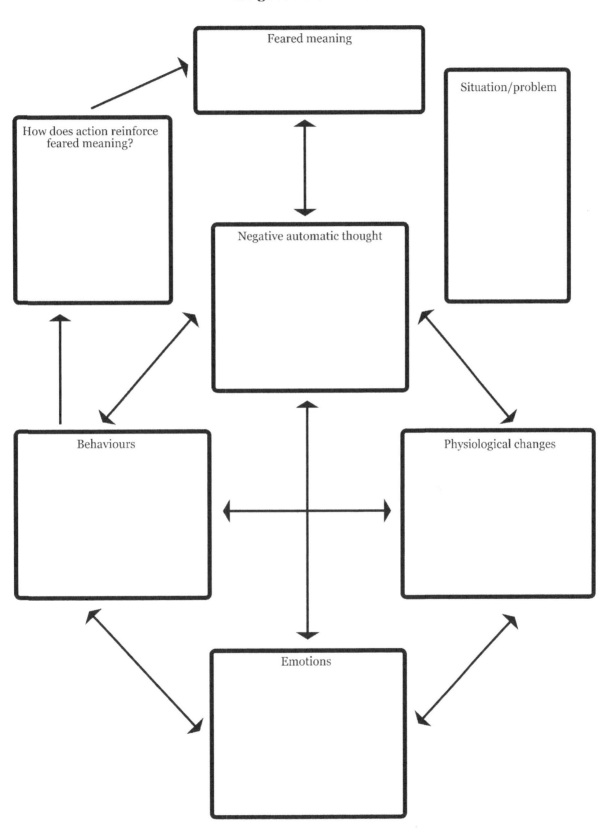

The generic CBT model

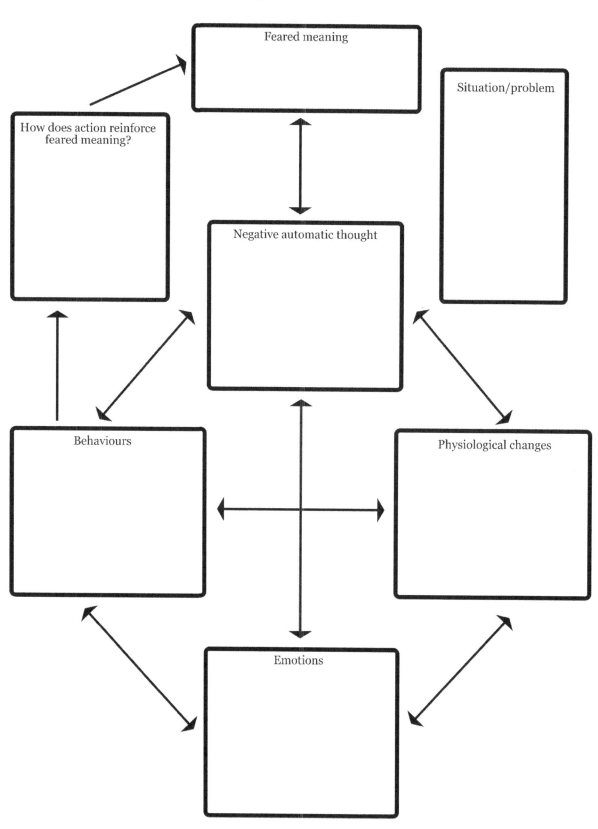

The generic CBT model

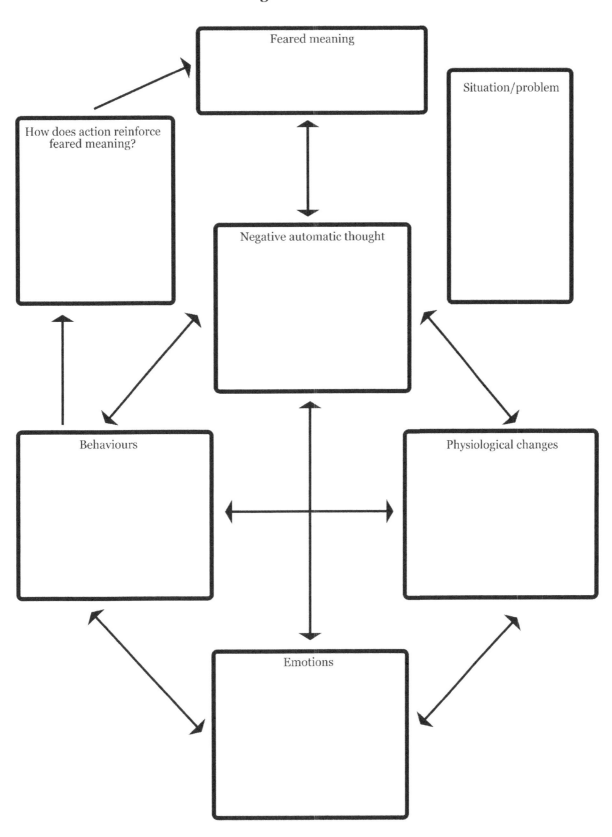

The generic CBT model

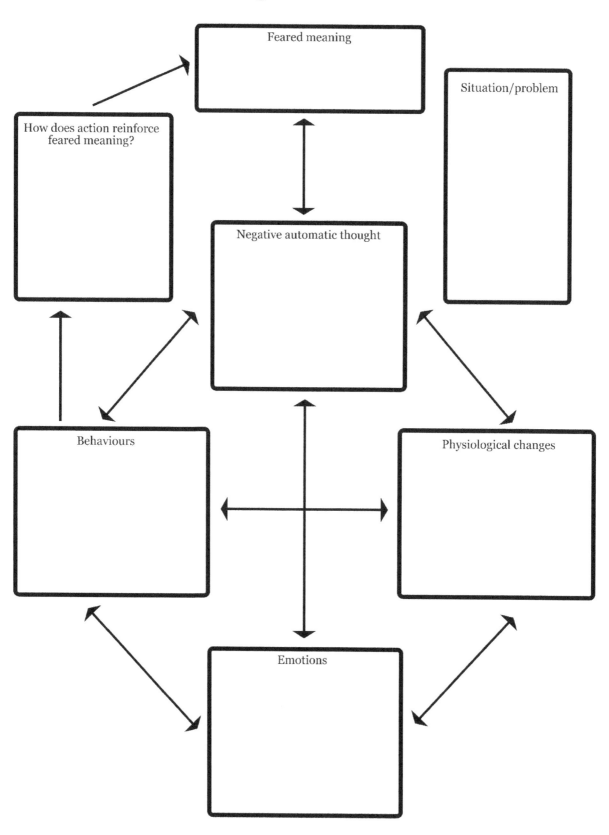

The generic CBT model

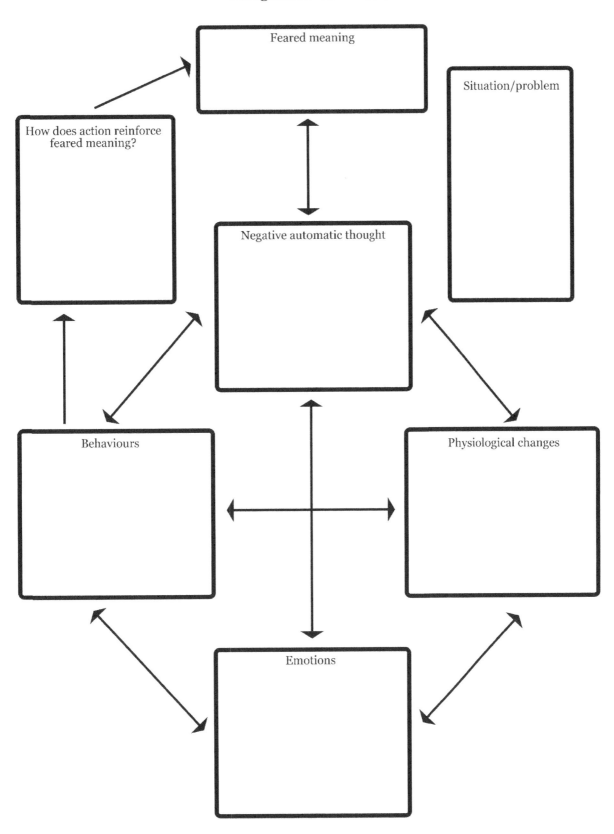

Thoughts, feelings and behaviour cycle

A thoughts, feelings and behaviour cycle is perhaps the best starting point to find out how CBT models work. Writing down your thoughts, feelings and behaviours and placing them in cycles, such as the one shown below, will increase your ability to be self-observant. The process of self-observation alone can have a big impact on your thinking processes and speed up your recovery from mental health problems. This simple cycle is designed to help you recognise that thoughts can have a significant impact on emotion: emotions can influence behaviour, and behaviour can determine thoughts and feelings. Although this cycle will not resolve your difficulties, it will increase your awareness of your problems, and this will increase your motivation to make changes.

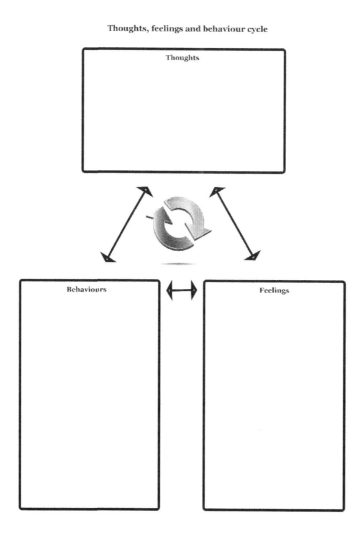

Thoughts, feelings and behaviour cycle

Thoughts

Behaviours

Feelings

Thoughts, feelings and behaviour cycle

Thoughts

'She cancelled our appointment deliberately because she does not like working with me'

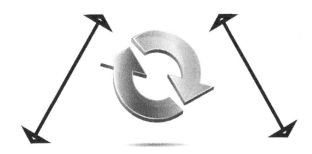

Behaviours

Become slightly more hostile, distant and dismissive

Feelings

Feel irritated and angry

Thoughts, feelings and behaviour cycle

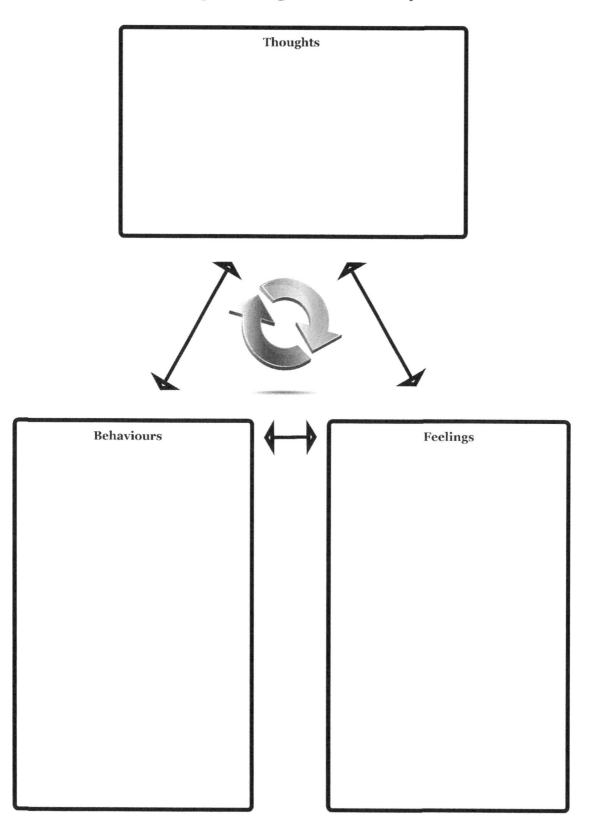

Thoughts

Behaviours

Feelings

A model of social anxiety

CBT models of social anxiety suggest that a social anxiety experience starts with an initial or triggering situation that can activate an individual's beliefs and assumptions. If you experience social anxiety, beliefs or fears may become active before, during or after a social situation. A natural tendency if you are socially anxious is to attempt to get rid of or hide your anxiety. You may also carry out safety behaviours, with the most commonly used behaviours being self-focus and self-preoccupation. The use of safety behaviours generally leads to increased symptoms of social anxiety. You may then use your struggle to cope with your anxiety in social situations and use that as further evidence for your beliefs and assumptions.

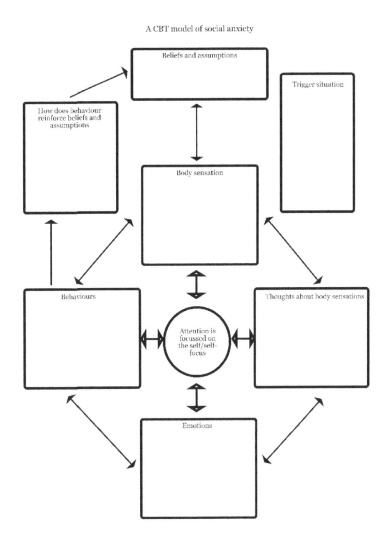

A CBT model of social anxiety

A CBT model of social anxiety

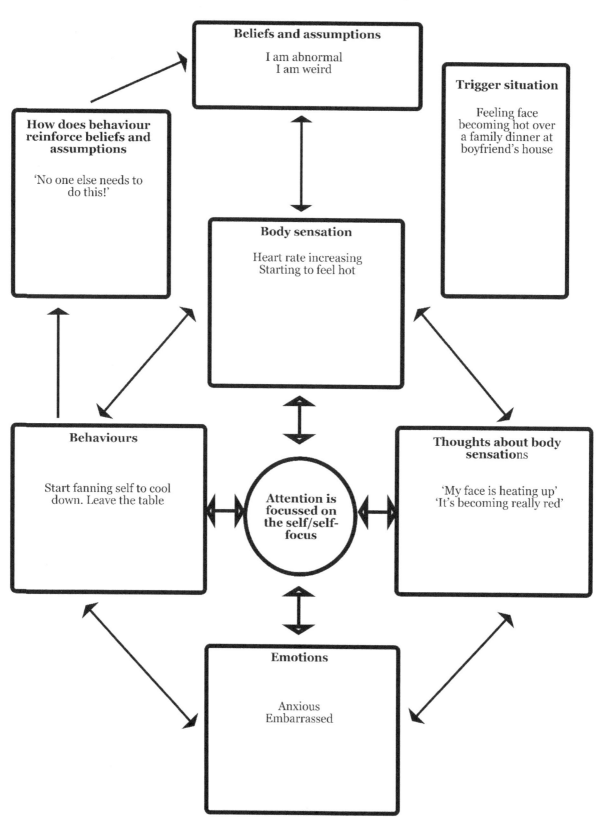

Copied from *Breaking Free from Social Anxiety*

A CBT model of social anxiety

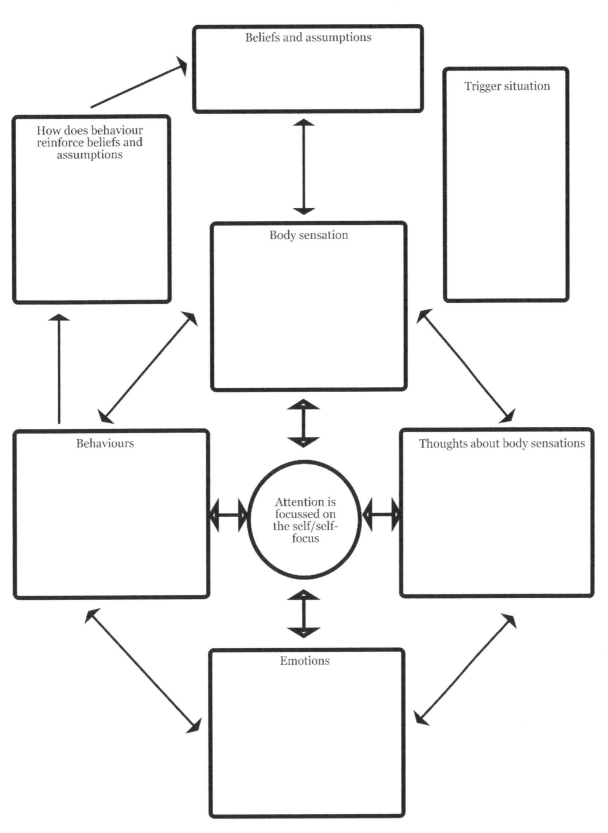

The vicious flower model (Moorey, 2010; Wilson & Veale, 2009)

The vicious flower model is probably best known for its use with health anxiety. If you are experiencing health anxiety, your anxiety may be triggered by intrusive thoughts about illness, and you might find yourself carrying out safety behaviours to help yourself feel better. These safety behaviours may include monitoring your body for signs of illness; seeking reassurance from your doctor; going onto the internet and researching symptoms; worrying about how you might cope with serious illness; and requesting medical tests or investigations. Sometimes, however, the very behaviours that we use to feel safe can actually make us feel more anxious and we end up feeling even more pre-occupied with a search for signs and symptoms of illness. The vicious flower model is used as an analogy to explain how the habits that we use can end up making us feel worse. The vicious flower is a bit like a poisonous foxglove. The flower may be tempting to look at and touch, but if you pick up the petals and start playing around with them you may end up poisoning yourself.

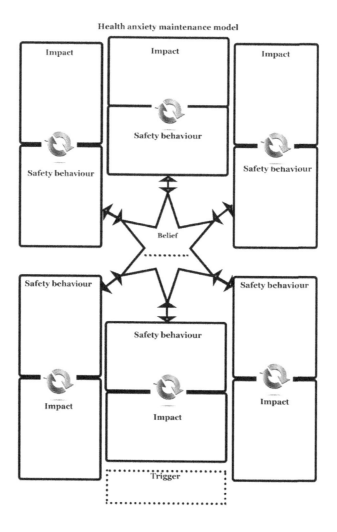

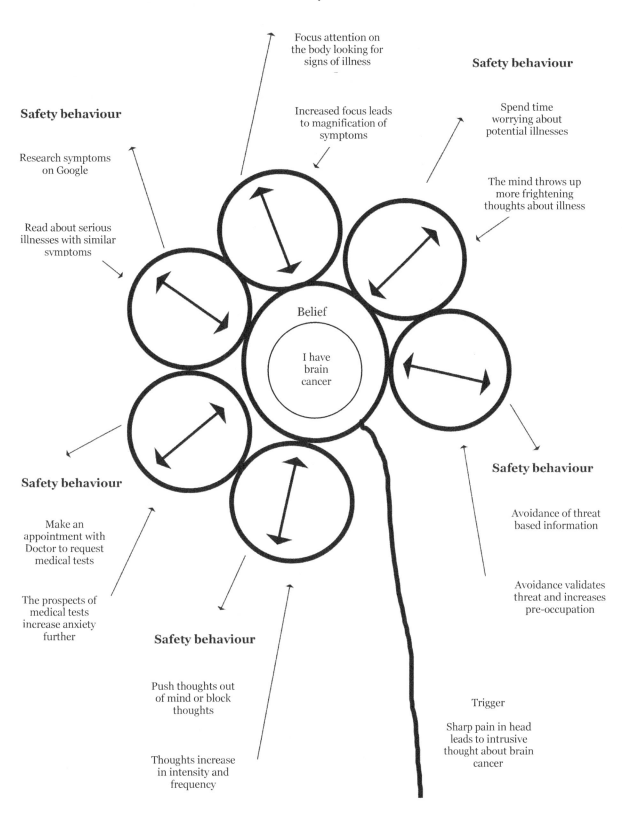

Vicious flower model, adapted from Moorey, 2010; Wilson & Veale, 2009

Safety behaviour

Focus attention on the body looking for signs of illness

Increased focus leads to magnification of symptoms

Safety behaviour

Spend time worrying about potential illnesses

The mind throws up more frightening thoughts about illness

Safety behaviour

Research symptoms on Google

Read about serious illnesses with similar symptoms

Belief

I have brain cancer

Safety behaviour

Make an appointment with Doctor to request medical tests

The prospects of medical tests increase anxiety further

Safety behaviour

Push thoughts out of mind or block thoughts

Thoughts increase in intensity and frequency

Safety behaviour

Avoidance of threat based information

Avoidance validates threat and increases pre-occupation

Trigger

Sharp pain in head leads to intrusive thought about brain cancer

Health anxiety maintenance model

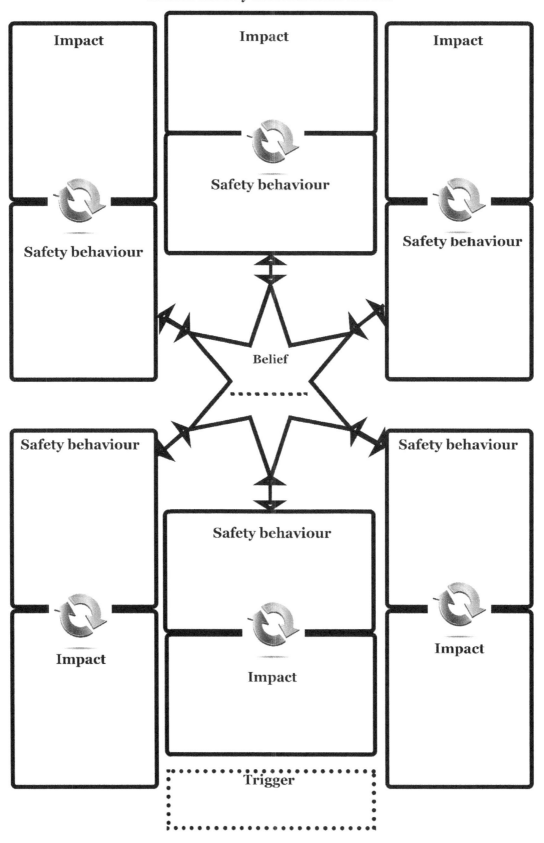

The OCD model of anxiety (Rachman, Coughtrey, Shafran, & Radomsky, 2014)

At its heart, Rachman et al.'s OCD model of anxiety brings to awareness that it is our reaction to intrusive thoughts that is the most significant factor in the maintenance of OCD. Research has found that most people have intrusive thoughts, but can easily dismiss them as 'just thoughts' (Abramowitz et al, 2014). However, people with OCD find it very difficult to do this, and often use their thoughts as evidence that something bad has happened or is going to happen. Rachman et al.'s model begins with a trigger, that may occur in your environment: for example, walking past a used condom on the street. Triggers will obviously be different depending on how your OCD manifests itself. Common among all sufferers of OCD is that environmental triggers bring **intrusive thoughts** to mind. An intrusive thought is a thought that pushes its way into awareness with extreme urgency. Intrusive thoughts often appear to come out of nowhere, carrying high levels of emotional distress with them.

Rachman et al.'s model draws attention to how intrusive thoughts are interpreted, especially if you sometimes use your intrusive thoughts as evidence that something dangerous has happened, something awful might happen, or that there is something seriously wrong with you for having such a thought. If you have OCD you may

attempt to neutralise or get rid of intense emotion by carrying out a neutralising behaviour or by avoiding certain things. The neutralising action or avoidance behaviour reinforces the fear of the initial stimuli through a process called **negative reinforcement**. Negative reinforcement occurs when you carry out certain behaviours to remove painful feelings. Over time, as processes are repeated and memory pathways are laid down, you may even begin to carry out certain safety behaviours automatically, without thinking.

OCD model of anxiety adapted from Rachman, S., Coughtrey, A., Shafran, R., & Radomsky, A. (2014)

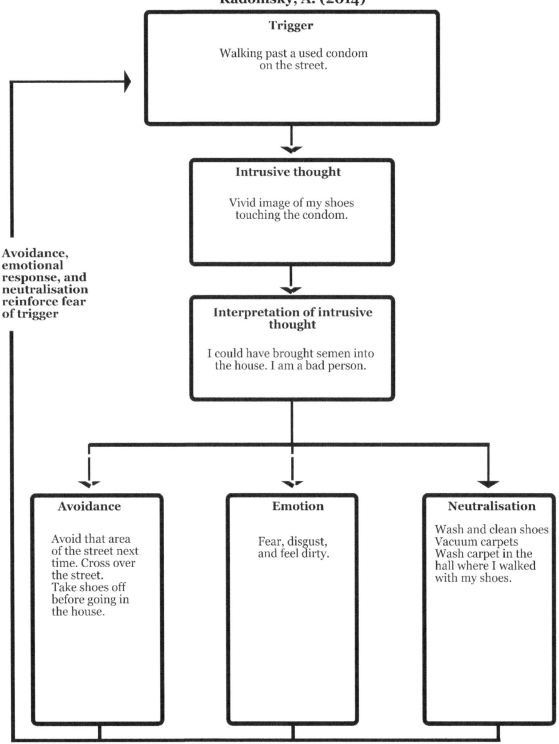

Trigger

Walking past a used condom
on the street.

Intrusive thought

Vivid image of my shoes
touching the condom.

Interpretation of intrusive thought

I could have brought semen into
the house. I am a bad person.

Avoidance, emotional response, and neutralisation reinforce fear of trigger

Avoidance

Avoid that area
of the street next
time. Cross over
the street.
Take shoes off
before going in
the house.

Emotion

Fear, disgust,
and feel dirty.

Neutralisation

Wash and clean shoes
Vacuum carpets
Wash carpet in the
hall where I walked
with my shoes.

Alternate OCD model

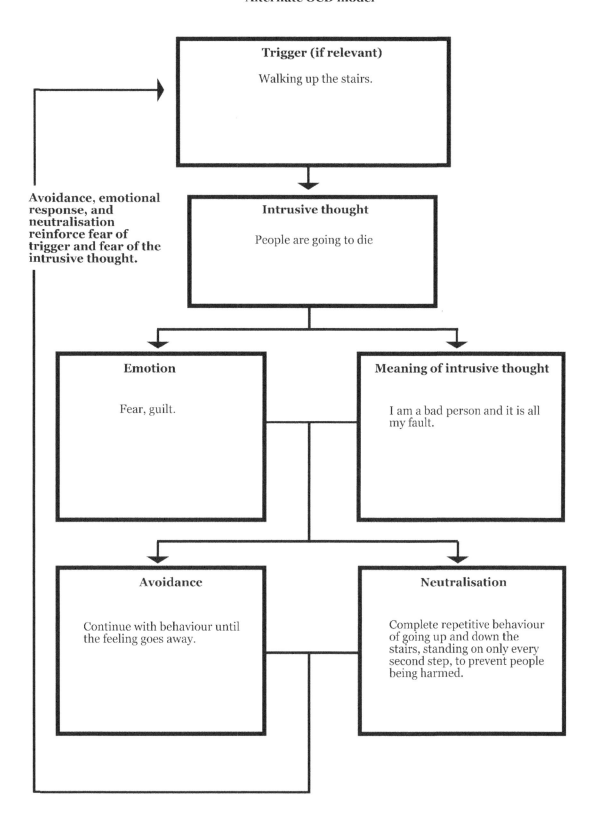

Trigger (if relevant)

Walking up the stairs.

Avoidance, emotional response, and neutralisation reinforce fear of trigger and fear of the intrusive thought.

Intrusive thought

People are going to die

Emotion

Fear, guilt.

Meaning of intrusive thought

I am a bad person and it is all my fault.

Avoidance

Continue with behaviour until the feeling goes away.

Neutralisation

Complete repetitive behaviour of going up and down the stairs, standing on only every second step, to prevent people being harmed.

Alternate OCD model

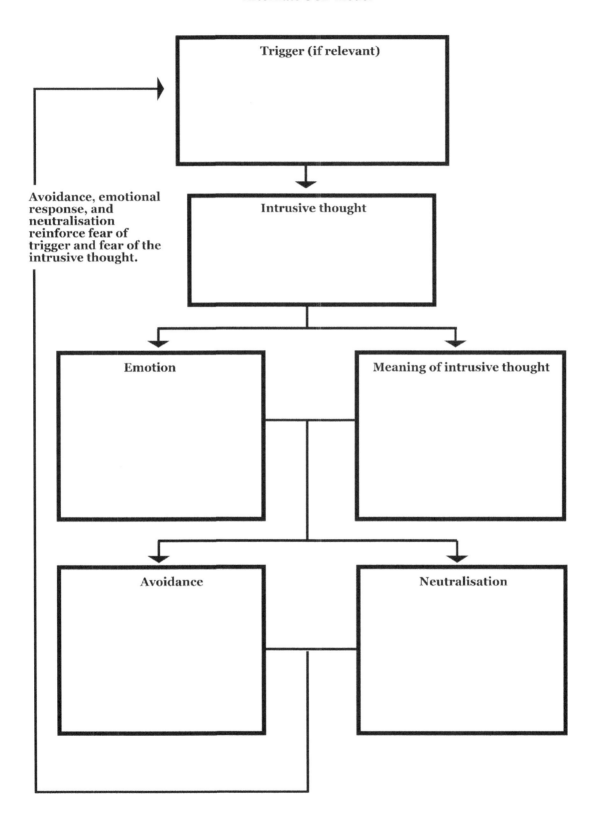

Standard OCD model

Intrusive thoughts

Thought of sexually assaulting a child.

Trigger situation

A child brushing past me.

Emotions and physiological symptoms

Fear, disgust, agitation.

Feel tense, on edge.

Neutralising action

Try to block thought by trying to think of something else.

Say 'I'm not a paedophile' in my head.

Standard OCD model

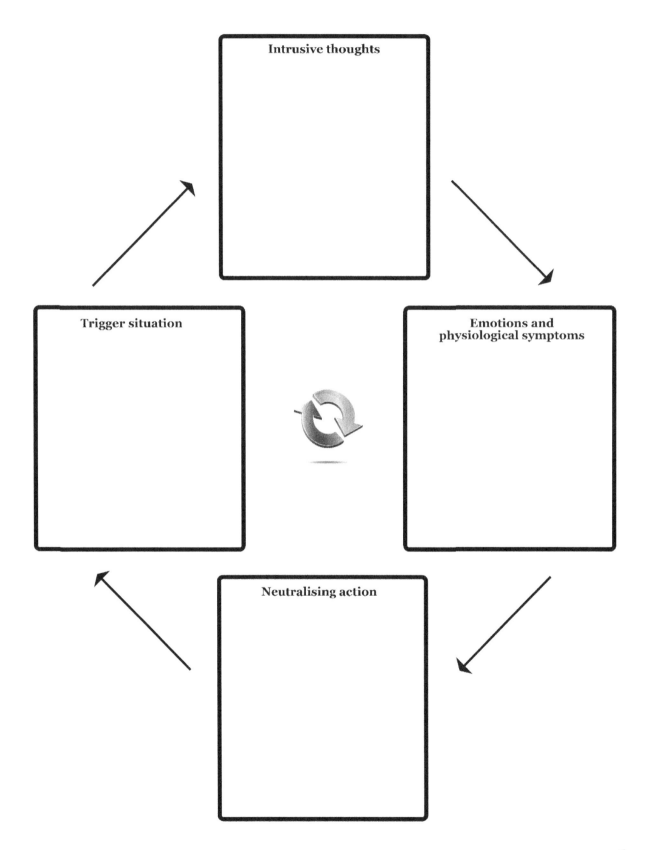

Clark's panic model (Clark 1986)

The main feature of David Clark's 1986 panic model that distinguishes it from other CBT maintenance cycles is that it includes catastrophic misinterpretations of symptoms of anxiety. Increased focus on specific symptoms of anxiety leads to magnification of symptoms. This means that when you are experiencing panic symptoms you may find yourself focusing on symptoms in your body, and using your symptoms as evidence to support your deepest fears, whether this is an idea that you are experiencing a heart attack, having a stroke, going insane, or losing control etc. The pre-frontal cortex, an area of the brain just below the neo-cortex, at the front of the brain, tends to shut down in panic, leaving primitive (sub-cortical) regions of the brain more dominant. Dominance of the primitive regions of the brain will leave your mind unable to access logical, analytic thought. When this occurs you will find that you have an increased tendency towards carrying out habitual behaviour – or in other words, doing what you have always done before. The final result can be that you experience panic cycles repetitively, which can feel exhausting and draining on your body.

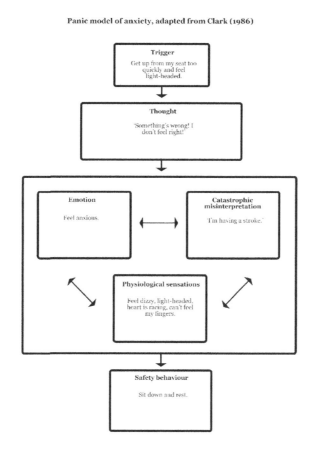

Panic model of anxiety, adapted from Clark (1986)

Panic model of anxiety, adapted from Clark (1986)

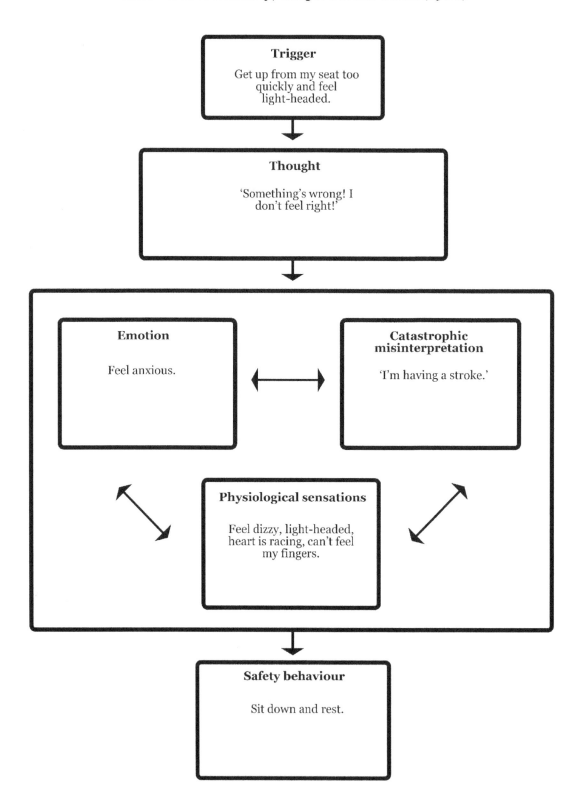

A CBT model for panic (from *A Journey With Panic*)

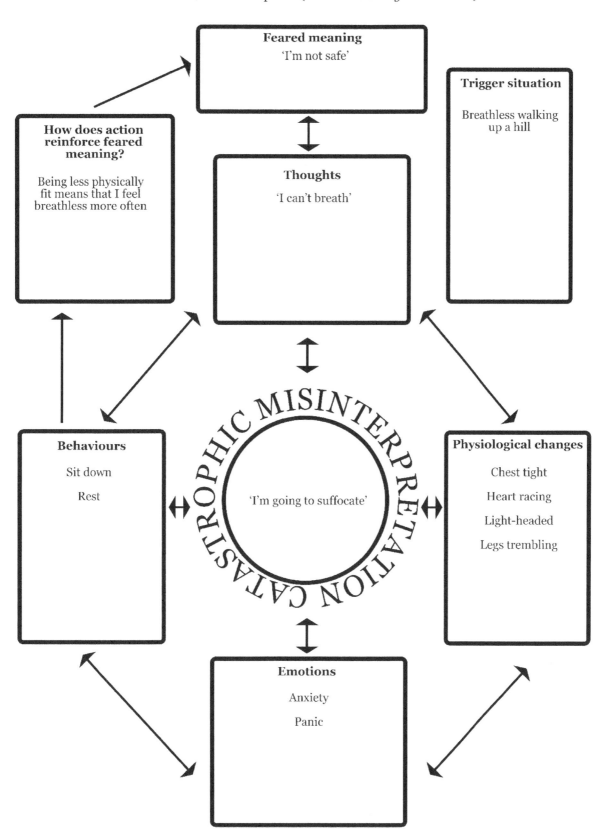

A CBT model for panic (from *A Journey With Panic*)

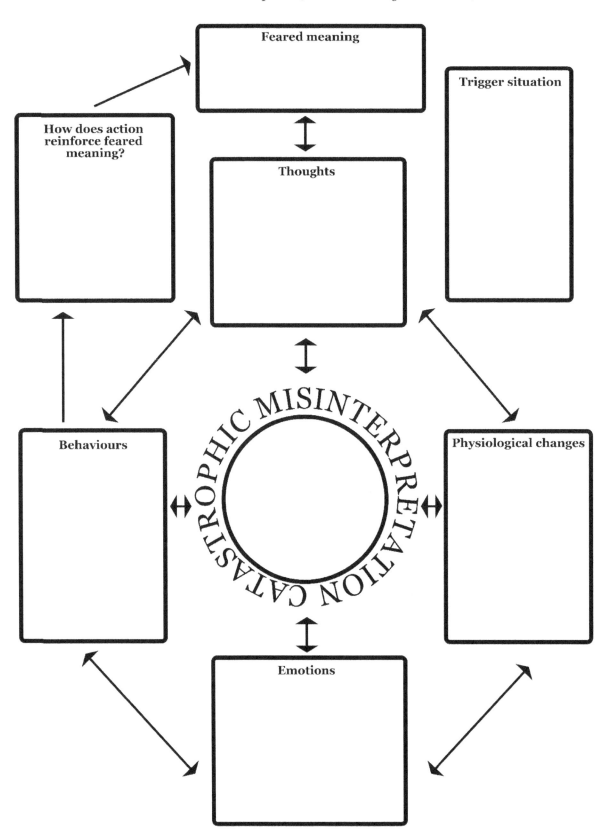

Manning & Ridgeway's self-phobic model (Manning & Ridgeway, 2015)

Clark's CBT model works very well to explain panic. However, several individuals feel panicky but do not come close to experiencing a full scale panic attack. It is more difficult to apply panic models in such cases. Many individuals are hyper-vigilant to their bodily reactions and often take action quite quickly in an attempt to control their body's reactions. This can result in individuals a) excessively monitoring their body in a pre-emptive fashion; for example, recording their blood pressure and pulse and b) becoming increasingly avoidant of activities that may result in a change in their body state; for example, not engaging in exercise as it results in a heart rate increase. The whole process leads to an increase in a) self-vigilance, and b) fear of one's own body's reactions. Problems are maintained as a result of an increase in phobic reactions to one's own body reactions.

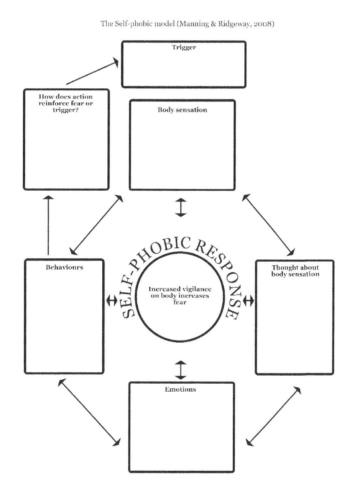

The Self-phobic model (Manning & Ridgeway, 2008)

The Self-phobic model (Manning & Ridgeway, 2008)

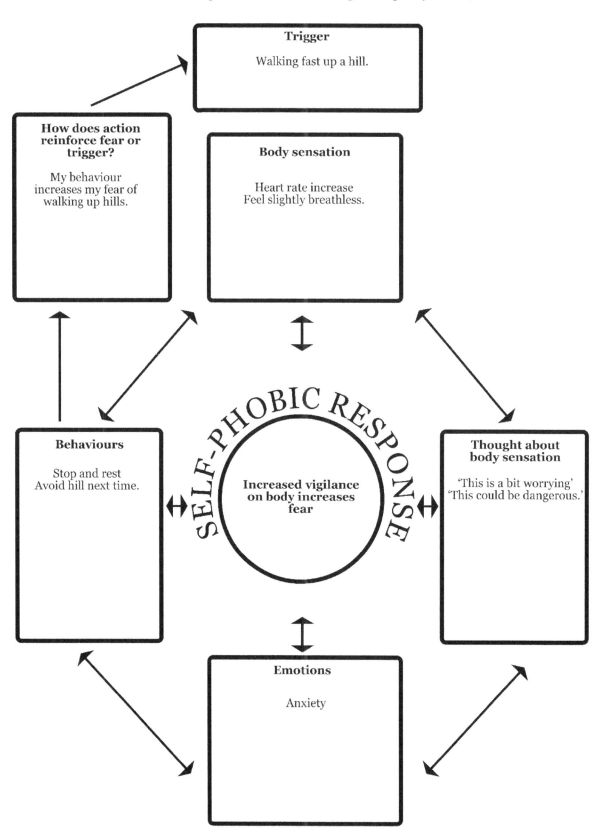

Trigger

Walking fast up a hill.

How does action reinforce fear or trigger?

My behaviour increases my fear of walking up hills.

Body sensation

Heart rate increase
Feel slightly breathless.

SELF-PHOBIC RESPONSE

Increased vigilance on body increases fear

Behaviours

Stop and rest
Avoid hill next time.

Thought about body sensation

'This is a bit worrying'
'This could be dangerous.'

Emotions

Anxiety

The Self-phobic model (Manning & Ridgeway, 2008)

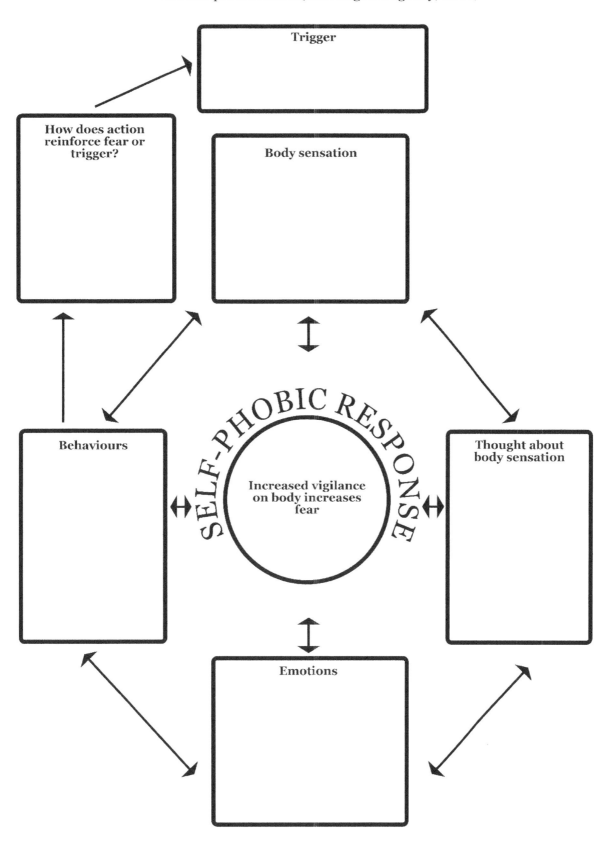

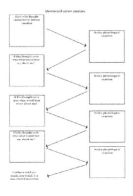

Chapter 7 The downward arrow

The downward arrow exercise is commonly used in CBT. In its simplest form it is designed to help you access your core beliefs. Core beliefs are initially very difficult to identify and it is natural that you will put up psychological resistance to accessing them, due to the fact that retrieving them will be distressing.

The downward arrow exercise is a very difficult exercise to complete by yourself. It can produce high levels of emotional distress and will involve you accessing your deepest fears. Understandably, most people feel an aversion to completing a downward arrow exercise alone, and it is often easier to do it with a therapist.

To start the exercise bring one of your most painful negative automatic thoughts to your awareness. Scan your body while you hold a NAT in awareness and notice the impact that your thought has on you at an emotional or physiological level.

Focussing on your feeling ask yourself – 'If this thought were true what would it say or mean about me?' Repeat this questioning process with each progressive thought that your mind produces until you find yourself repeating earlier thoughts. When your thoughts become most painful or aversive you are likely to be accessing a belief. Beliefs are judgemental, unconditional statements about the self or others beginning with the word I or others. For example, 'I am bad', 'I am worthless', 'I am inadequate', 'I am weak' and, 'Others cannot be trusted'.

Downward arrow exercise

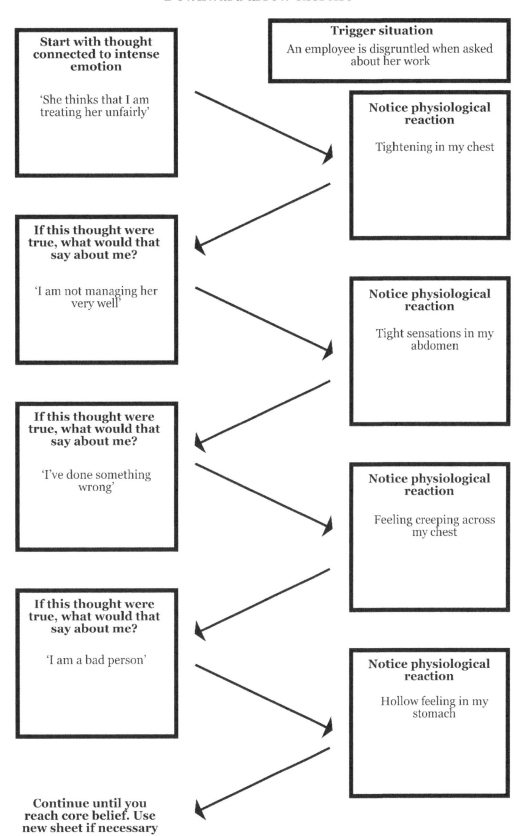

Trigger situation
An employee is disgruntled when asked about her work

Start with thought connected to intense emotion

'She thinks that I am treating her unfairly'

Notice physiological reaction

Tightening in my chest

If this thought were true, what would that say about me?

'I am not managing her very well'

Notice physiological reaction

Tight sensations in my abdomen

If this thought were true, what would that say about me?

'I've done something wrong'

Notice physiological reaction

Feeling creeping across my chest

If this thought were true, what would that say about me?

'I am a bad person'

Notice physiological reaction

Hollow feeling in my stomach

Continue until you reach core belief. Use new sheet if necessary

Downward arrow exercise

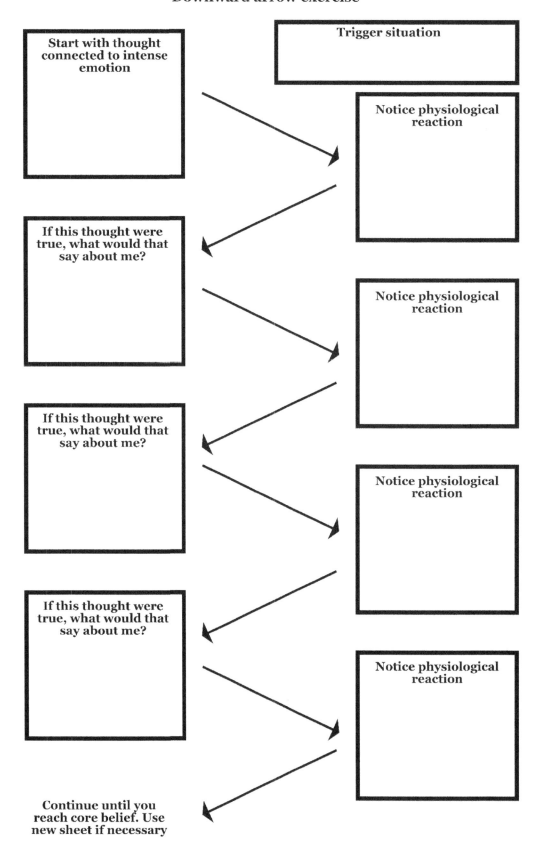

Start with thought connected to intense emotion

Trigger situation

Notice physiological reaction

If this thought were true, what would that say about me?

Notice physiological reaction

If this thought were true, what would that say about me?

Notice physiological reaction

If this thought were true, what would that say about me?

Notice physiological reaction

Continue until you reach core belief. Use new sheet if necessary

Downward arrow exercise

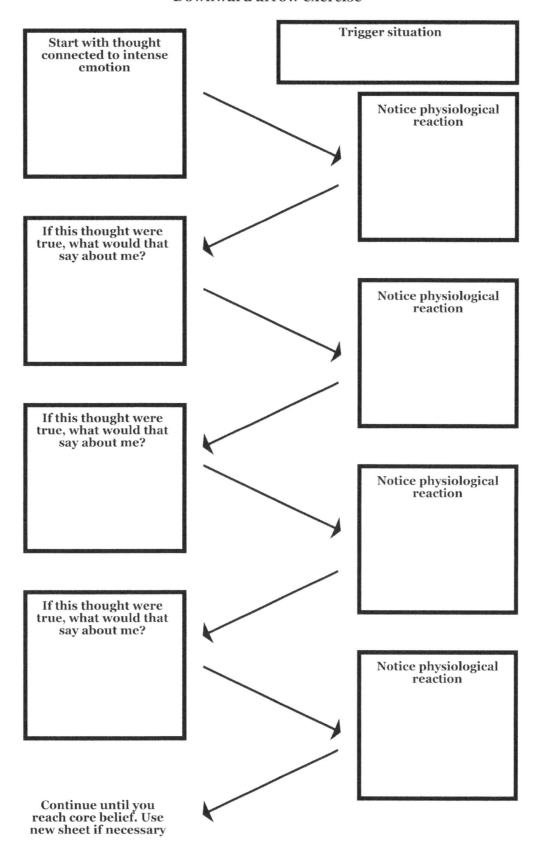

Start with thought connected to intense emotion

Trigger situation

Notice physiological reaction

If this thought were true, what would that say about me?

Notice physiological reaction

If this thought were true, what would that say about me?

Notice physiological reaction

If this thought were true, what would that say about me?

Notice physiological reaction

Continue until you reach core belief. Use new sheet if necessary

Downward arrow exercise

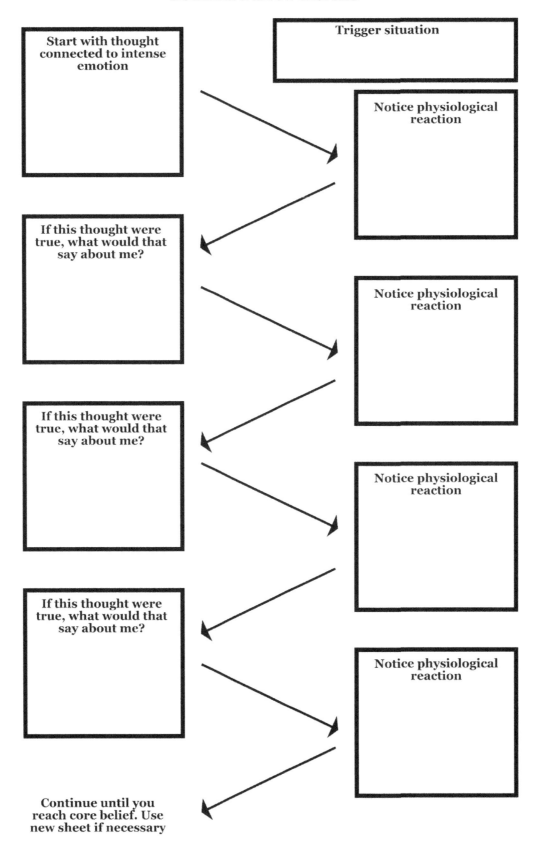

Start with thought connected to intense emotion

Trigger situation

Notice physiological reaction

If this thought were true, what would that say about me?

Notice physiological reaction

If this thought were true, what would that say about me?

Notice physiological reaction

If this thought were true, what would that say about me?

Notice physiological reaction

Continue until you reach core belief. Use new sheet if necessary

Downward arrow exercise

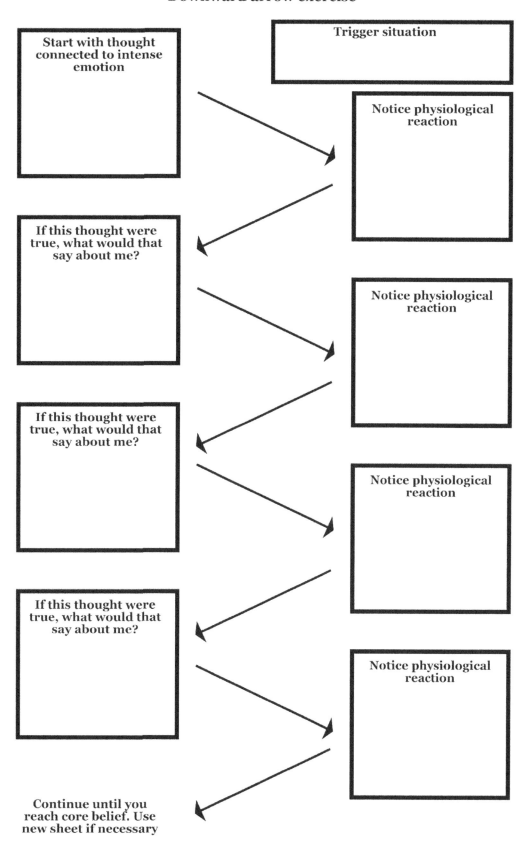

Start with thought connected to intense emotion

Trigger situation

Notice physiological reaction

If this thought were true, what would that say about me?

Notice physiological reaction

If this thought were true, what would that say about me?

Notice physiological reaction

If this thought were true, what would that say about me?

Notice physiological reaction

Continue until you reach core belief. Use new sheet if necessary

Downward arrow exercise

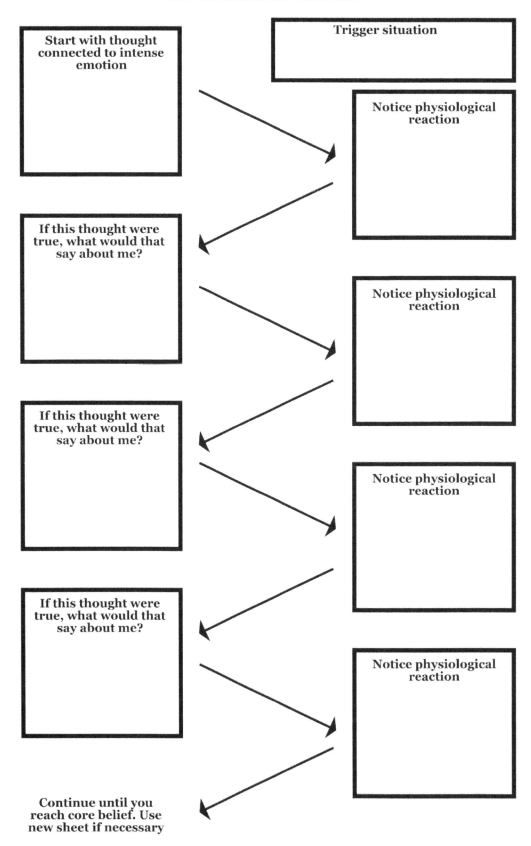

Trigger situation

Start with thought connected to intense emotion

Notice physiological reaction

If this thought were true, what would that say about me?

Notice physiological reaction

If this thought were true, what would that say about me?

Notice physiological reaction

If this thought were true, what would that say about me?

Notice physiological reaction

Continue until you reach core belief. Use new sheet if necessary

Downward arrow exercise

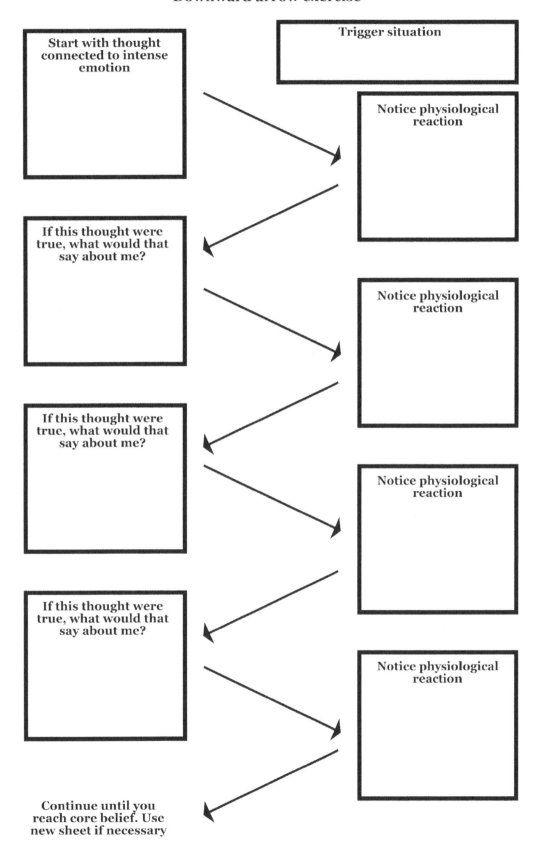

Chapter 8
NAT
challenging

The NAT challenging form is incredibly useful in CBT. It is best used with thoughts that produce more intense emotions. After you have completed a thought record look through your thoughts and select one that produces an intense feeling.

Write down as much evidence for the thought as possible. After you have written down your evidence *for* the thought, in the next column write down as much evidence *against* the thought as possible. Sometimes it can be useful to ask others or your CBT therapist to help you with evidence against thoughts. After you have completed both columns, write down a more balanced thought. A balanced thought may reflect both the evidence for and against the thought. Once you have your balanced thought run it through in your mind and assess how you feel emotionally and physically.

NAT challenging form

Frightening automatic thought, for example, 'I am going to die.'	Evidence for negative automatic thought, for example, 'I feel that it might happen.'	Evidence against negative automatic thought, for example, 'This has never happened before.'	New more balanced thought, for example, 'Although I feel panicky nothing has happened in the past and is unlikely to happen this time.'
'She thinks that I am treating her unfairly.'	She changed her mind about what we had agreed very suddenly. I felt a negative vibe from her text. I feel that she doesn't like me and thinks that I am a mean person.	She is out of her depth about what we agreed and is finding it difficult to manage. Although she changed her mind she is still friendly and positive. I cannot read people's minds and they have their own reasons for doing things that are not about me. She has not said that she has been treated unfairly.	'She changed her mind, and I have a habit of taking that kind of thing personally, but people have their own reasons for making their decisions that are nothing to do with me.'

NAT challenging form

Frightening automatic thought, for example, 'I am going to die.'	Evidence for negative automatic thought, for example, 'I feel that it might happen.'	Evidence against negative automatic thought, for example, 'This has never happened before.'	New more balanced thought, for example, 'Although I feel panicky nothing has happened in the past and is unlikely to happen this time.'

NAT challenging form

Frightening automatic thought, for example, 'I am going to die.'	Evidence for negative automatic thought, for example, 'I feel that it might happen.'	Evidence against negative automatic thought, for example, 'This has never happened before.'	New more balanced thought, for example, 'Although I feel panicky nothing has happened in the past and is unlikely to happen this time.'

NAT challenging form

Frightening automatic thought, for example, 'I am going to die.'	Evidence for negative automatic thought, for example, 'I feel that it might happen.'	Evidence against negative automatic thought, for example, 'This has never happened before.'	New more balanced thought, for example, 'Although I feel panicky nothing has happened in the past and is unlikely to happen this time.'

NAT challenging form

Frightening automatic thought, for example, 'I am going to die.'	Evidence for negative automatic thought, for example, 'I feel that it might happen.'	Evidence against negative automatic thought, for example, 'This has never happened before.'	New more balanced thought, for example, 'Although I feel panicky nothing has happened in the past and is unlikely to happen this time.'

Chapter 9
Belief and rule challenging

Core beliefs and rules are very difficult to challenge and it is highly likely that part of you will cling onto them tightly. Beliefs can feel like fixed truths and it often seems as if they simply cannot be contested. Many of us spend huge amounts of our time, (perhaps even changing the way we live our lives), attempting to prove them wrong. We may also develop self-imposed rules about our behaviour in order to compensate against them.

Within the field of CBT, beliefs are directly connected to self-imposed conditions of worth or compensations. For example, the belief 'I am bad' could be associated with the rule: 'If people approve of me and I am able to help others at all times then I will be OK.' Dropping our beliefs can feel quite frightening, as in most cases we will have devoted huge amounts of time and resources to compensating against them. Beliefs can feel as though they are part of us and sometimes we might feel that we could lose part of our identity without them. Beliefs have the power to impact on our relationships, our choice of partner and occupation. There are no areas of our lives that are untouched by our beliefs.

The belief and rule challenging exercises that follow are predominantly designed to bring your beliefs and rules into awareness. These exercises are not powerful enough on their own to change or to destabilise beliefs and rules, but they may make your beliefs and rules slightly more malleable/flexible.

Belief challenging exercise

Belief
I am bad

How real and familiar does the belief feel?

It feels real a lot of the time. It feels as though it is part of me.

What impact does that belief have on your life?

I feel that I have to keep doing things to keep people happy. If people are pleased with me I feel OK for a little while. As soon as anyone complains about anything I feel as though things are my fault and I need to fix it. It stops me handling criticism well and I end up taking on too much responsibility.

What benefits does this belief have on your life?

I guess that it does help me to help others and make a difference to others in their lives. I work in a helping profession.

Were you born with that belief?

No.

How old is the belief?

About 45 years old.

Where do you think the belief came from?

I think I learnt it from my father or maybe from school as a child.

If you learnt the belief from a person, where do you think he or she learnt it from?

If it was my father he probably learnt it from painful experiences that he had as a child.

Do you want to keep that belief?

No. I think no matter how much I do it is there anyway. Normally there is at least one person at one point in time that who is unhappy with me.

If you gave yourself an opportunity to believe something else, what belief would you pick?

I am the same as everybody else.

How do you think you might feel if you choose to believe your new belief as much as the old one?

I would feel a lot more relaxed. (But part of me feels that I am not allowed to believe that I am the same as everyone else.)

How does knowing that you can choose to believe something else make you feel?

When I think that I can be the same as everyone else I have an unusual experience of liberation.

Belief challenging exercise

Belief

How real and familiar does the belief feel?

What impact does that belief have on your life?

What benefits does this belief have on your life?

Were you born with that belief?

How old is the belief?

Where do you think the belief came from?

If you learnt the belief from a person, where do you think he or she learnt it from?

Do you want to keep that belief?

If you gave yourself an opportunity to believe something else, what belief would you pick?

How do you think you might feel if you choose to believe your new belief as much as the old one?

How does knowing that you can choose to believe something else make you feel?

Rule challenging exercise

Rule If others are happy with me then I will be OK.

How real and familiar does the rule feel?

It feels real a lot of the time. It feels as though it is part of me.

What impact does the rule have on your life?

A lot of my goals are focussed on things I need to do to keep other people happy.

It makes me easy to manipulate and once people realise I am like that they will often use it to make me feel bad so that I will do what they want.

What benefits does this rule have on your life?

Generally, most people seem to be unhappy with me at some point so I guess it just makes me feel miserable.

Were you born with that rule?

No.

How old is the rule?

I guess about 40 years old.

Where do you think the rule came from?

I learnt it from my parents.

If you learnt the rule from a person, where do you think he or she learnt it from?

I think my parents learnt it from their parents. It seems to be stronger on my father's side of the family.

Do you want to keep that rule?

Definitely not.

If you gave yourself an opportunity to have another rule, what rule would you pick?

Other people are responsible for their own happiness. I am responsible for my happiness. I can help others, or give advice to others, but they are responsible for their own feelings.

How do you think you might feel if you choose to believe your new rule as much as the old one?

I would feel as though I am not continually failing to please others. I would feel more relaxed.

How does knowing that you can choose to have another rule make you feel?

It feels a little alien. It feels a little hard-hearted. But, I feel better because I know logically this will create less stress and I will feel better and it will actually be more beneficial to others in the long-term.

Rule challenging exercise

Rule

How real and familiar does the rule feel?

How old is the rule?

If you gave yourself an opportunity to have another rule, what rule would you pick?

What impact does the rule have on your life?

Where do you think the rule came from?

How do you think you might feel if you choose to believe your new rule as much as the old one?

If you learnt the rule from a person, where do you think he or she learnt it from?

What benefits does this rule have on your life?

How does knowing that you can choose to have another rule make you feel?

Do you want to keep that rule?

Were you born with that rule?

Future most developed self exercise - Sheet 1

Describe how you filter your own choices, what most excites you, and the way life may unfold?

What do you want out of life from a list like to become?

How you look/appearance:

Describe posture and body language:

How do you think/feel/behave to act - in history, today and future/now:

How do you react and feel/act, it would relate ongoing?

How do you react and feel/act, it would relate to you?

Chapter 10
The future most developed self exercise

The FMDS exercise is designed to help you focus on the person that you intend to become someday. It is a self in the future: a person who you will become when you have made all of the changes that you feel that you need to make; a person who is in charge about how they live their daily life. This self has all of the necessary inner resources (e.g., compassion, kindness, etc.) and coping strategies to make the most of his or her life.

The best place to start when using this exercise is to select a problem that you have experienced just lately. This will be a problem involving at least one other person. It will be a problem that you feel you have not handled very well. Even now when you think about it, you will be unsure how you could have handled things differently. Run that problem through in your mind and assess how you dealt with it and think about how you felt afterwards. Now scan your body and notice the various uncomfortable feelings that you are experiencing.

Complete the following FMDS exercise with your therapist. Do whatever you need to do to keep the image of your FMDS in mind. Think about the way she/he looks, thinks, feels and behaves. Once you have completed the construction of your FMDS image, step inside your FMDS and watch from inside your FMDS as she/he resolves your problem for you on your behalf. Bear in mind that when your FMDS is solving your problem for you, your everyday self (i.e., the self inside your FMDS) will be a passive observer and will not do or say anything. The everyday self will simply be watching, listening and feeling how the FMDS feels and noticing what the FMDS does.

Once your FMDS has resolved your problem, step outside of your FMDS and assess how your FMDS may have viewed or reacted to your problem differently.

Future most developed self exercise – Sheet 1

What are the main differences between your future most developed self and the way that you are today?

He has more grey hair. He has an improved posture. He appears more serene. He appears lighter in weight and looks physically healthy. He appears more spiritually aware.

What do you notice from what you see that this is the case?

I can see his grey hair. He holds himself better and looks calm. He looks unruffled as though he is taking the world in his stride. He looks young for his years.

Describe facial expression

He has a gentle smile. His brow is relaxed. He has open approachable, compassionate eyes.

Describe posture and body language

He holds himself in a mindful way. He has an open posture and is upright.

Describe hairstyle, physical appearance, clothing, footwear, makeup and jewellery etc

He is wearing loose-fitting natural fabrics. Light grey with possibly an Eastern feeling.

How does your 'future most developed self' sound when speaking?

He sounds calm and relaxed. He listens more than he speaks. He is softly spoken and gentle.

How does your 'future most developed self feel? Where in his/her body are these feelings experienced?

Calm and relaxed. He feels as though he is touch with the Universe. He feels these feelings in his chest, his arms, his legs, and his stomach.

Future most developed self exercise – Sheet 2

What do you notice about the way that your 'future most developed self' interacts with others?

Patient and kind. He uses thoughtful questions. He can still regress to his childhood with his friends. He is polite and he can be gregarious when he needs to be.

What does your 'future most developed self' believe about him/herself?

He has nothing to prove but he knows he can add a lot and he wants to do this. He knows that he has come a long way in his life and he lives his life with daily gratitude for that. He recognises how fortunate he is.

If your 'future most developed self' was asked what has led to her/him becoming the person that she/he currently is, what would he/she say?

Choose to spend more time in each moment. Approach each small moment with gratitude and love. Enjoy the experience of life and embrace the human experience.

Step inside your 'future most developed self.' How does it feel to be in her/his body?

Calm and connected with the Universe. Energy buzzing through the body.

Watch from beginning to end as your 'future most developed self' resolves a difficulty for you on your behalf.

What did you learn from your 'future most developed self?

He approaches helping others close to him in a kinaesthetic/healing way.

What do you make of the fact that the way that your 'future most developed self' resolved your problem all came from within you?

It's quite incredible. I feel as though I am evolving towards the person that I already am and letting go of the damage of previous generations.

Future most developed self exercise – Sheet 1

What are the main differences between your future most developed self and the way that you are today?

What do you notice from what you see that this is the case?

Describe facial expression

Describe posture and body language

Describe hairstyle, physical appearance, clothing, footwear, makeup and jewellery etc

How does your 'future most developed self' sound when speaking?

How does your 'future most developed self' feel? Where in his/her body are these feelings experienced?

Future most developed self exercise – Sheet 2

What do you notice about the way that your 'future most developed self' interacts with others?

What does your 'future most developed self' believe about him/herself?

If your 'future most developed self' was asked what has led to her/him becoming the person that she/he currently is, what would he/she say?

Step inside your 'future most developed self.' How does it feel to be in her/his body?

Watch from beginning to end as your 'future most developed self' resolves a difficulty for you on your behalf.

What did you learn from your 'future most developed self?

What do you make of the fact that the way that your 'future most developed self' resolved your problem all came from within you?

Future mood developed self exercise - Sheet 1

Think of the main title here, what do you think most developed self and the self that you are today?

What do you see when you imagine your life in future?

Describe held expression

Describe posture and body language

Describe (sketch physical experience clothing, texture, noise, sensations etc)

How does your future mood developed self stand when standing?

How does your future mood developed self walk?

Chapter 11
Behavioural
experiments

Behavioural experiments are a very important part of CBT. The general idea behind them is embedding positive behaviour change and breaking patterns of old maladaptive behaviour. To carry out a behavioural experiment we make a decision to change our behaviour and then put ourselves directly in a position to make that behaviour change happen. We make a prediction before the behaviour is carried out, (what we think or feel what might happen). We then carry out the behaviour and observe the results.

The majority of us make assumptions about how others might react to our behaviour, or how we might feel if we carry out a certain behaviour. A lot of the time, however, our assumptions are based on inaccurate information or a lack of knowledge. Behavioural experiments help with the development of **experiential knowledge**. Experiential knowledge is knowledge that can only be absorbed through personal experience. Experiential knowledge cannot be learned by thinking about issues or by reading a book.

Completing a behavioural experiment will involve you making a prediction about what you think may occur if you change your behaviour in a particular situation.

After you have made a prediction, carry out your new behaviour and observe what occurs. Behavioural experiments can be carried out in sessions with your CBT therapist or outside your sessions as homework.

Behavioural experiment sheet

Describe old behaviour or safety behaviour

Focus on myself to see how I am coming across.

Describe new behaviour
Focus externally.

How will you carry out new behaviour?

When I am in a social situation I will place my attention as much as possible on the other person. I will look at the other person and I will listen to what he or she has to say. If my mind turns inward to looking at myself I will spot this and without judging myself I will immediately shift my attention towards focussing externally.

Predictions about what will happen when you drop the safety behaviour. Write down as many scenarios as possible.

Looking at the other person will make him or her feel uncomfortable and this will make me feel more anxious. Alternatively, I may feel less anxious as I will not be focussing on myself. I have a memory of from when I was a child when somebody asked me what I staring at.

Carry out new behaviour and write down what actually happened here.

I found that I was actually much less anxious than I thought I would be. I did find myself shifting back to looking inwards a few times, but I noticed I was doing this and immediately started focussing externally once more. I found that overall I felt much more relaxed.

What did you learn from this process?
How likely are you to carry out this new behaviour again?

It was much easier than I thought. I felt much more relaxed. I am going to do this as much as possible going forwards now.

Behavioural experiment sheet

Describe old behaviour or safety behaviour

Describe new behaviour

How will you carry out new behaviour?

Predictions about what will happen when you drop the safety behaviour. Write down as many scenarios as possible.

Carry out new behaviour and write down what actually happened here.

What did you learn from this process?
How likely are you to carry out this new behaviour again?

Behavioural experiment sheet

Describe old behaviour or safety behaviour

Describe new behaviour

How will you carry out new behaviour?

Predictions about what will happen when you drop the safety behaviour. Write down as many scenarios as possible.

Carry out new behaviour and write down what actually happened here.

What did you learn from this process?
How likely are you to carry out this new behaviour again?

Behavioural experiment sheet

Describe old behaviour or safety behaviour

Describe new behaviour

How will you carry out new behaviour?

Predictions about what will happen when you drop the safety behaviour. Write down as many scenarios as possible.

Carry out new behaviour and write down what actually happened here.

What did you learn from this process?
How likely are you to carry out this new behaviour again?

Behavioural experiment sheet

Describe old behaviour or safety behaviour

Describe new behaviour

How will you carry out new behaviour?

Predictions about what will happen when you drop the safety behaviour. Write down as many scenarios as possible.

Carry out new behaviour and write down what actually happened here.

What did you learn from this process?
How likely are you to carry out this new behaviour again?

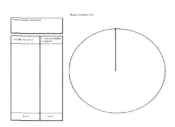

Chapter 12
Responsibility pies

Responsibility pies are very useful when we begin to take on too much responsibility for events in our lives where many other people are also involved, or when we have thoughts such as "It's all my fault!" If in discussion with your therapist you think that you are being overly responsible for an aspect of your life the first thing that you will need to do is to write down all of the people that are involved in the particular situation that you are working with. Place yourself at the bottom of the list. Assign a percentage of responsibility for everyone on the list leaving yourself until last.

Overleaf I have used an example of a football coach who is blaming herself for the poor performance of a team of youngsters that she is managing.

Responsibility Pie

Parents who did not bring their children to the match

Head coach

ME

Assistant coahces

The team

Children with behavioural problems

Parents of children with behavioural problems

Write down event here	
The team lost a match to a team in close competion	

People involved	% responsibility assigned
1. Parents who did not bring their children to the match	30%
2. Head coach for not assigning us more players and taking on all the new more experienced players	20%
3. Parents of children with behavioural problems	35%
4. The children with behavioural problems	5%
5. The team	2%
6. The assistant coaches	2%
7. Me	6%
Total	**100%**

Responsibility Pie

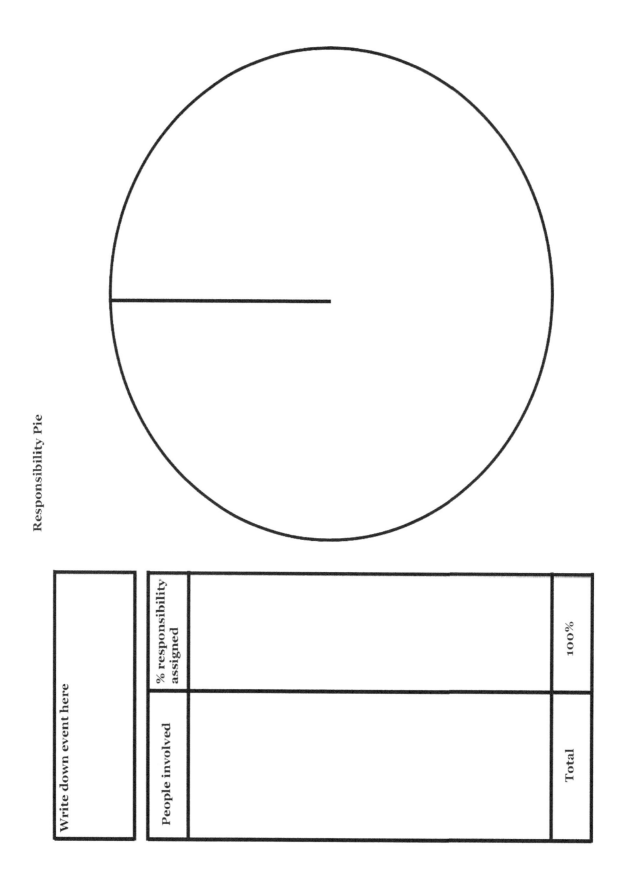

Write down event here	

People involved	% responsibility assigned
Total	100%

Responsibility pie

Chapter 13
A safe place

The use of a safe place generated by the mind is often helpful for people who have experienced painful events in their lives and are working through these events with their therapists.

Reminding yourself of your safe place when you are feeling distressed can reduce or soften the intensity of your emotions. Ideally, your safe place will be an outdoor place, (although it can also be indoors if no outdoor place feels safe). Outdoor place visualisations are preferable because these types of visualisations tend to bring about a better range of sensory information. It is generally best when designing a safe place to think of a place where you do not have any distinct memories involving others close to you. This is because using a safe place involving others can generate autobiographical memories (self-referent memories) that may then serve to distract you.

If finding a safe place is difficult, you can create an imaginary place with your therapist. You can, if you wish, also add a bridge to and from your safe place.

Safe place exercise – Page 1

Think of a place where you can go on your own. Ideally a place not connected with friends or relatives. An outdoor place where you feel safe and relaxed. Write down a brief description of your place below.

Park. Walking down a wood chip path, surrounded by trees.

Look ahead and notice the details of what you see. Write down what you see here. In particular, notice the details of what you see.

I can see a small piece of tree trunk. I can see the mud of the path with wood chip in some places. I can see the path ahead with several different varieties of trees. I can see nettles and wild flowers growing.

Look to your left and write down what you see. In particular notice the details of what you see.

To my left I can see a path veering towards the field. As I look through the trees I can make out a meandering river.

Look to your right and write down what you see. In particular notice the details of what you see.

To my right I can see weeds, small shrubs and more trees. I can see a short wooden fence, a drainage bank and then I can see a road in the distance.

Listen to the sounds that you hear. What do you notice?

I can hear a faint sound of rustling leaves. Maybe a slight vibration of traffic on a nearby road.

How do you feel when you hear these sounds?

Calm and relaxed.

Breathe in. What sensations to you notice in terms of how your breath feels? What does this place smell like?

I notice the air is fresh. There is a slight musty smell from warm wood chips baking in the sun.

Become aware of the air against your skin. What tells you from what you feel on your skin that you are in this place?

Cool all over. Mainly on my face and on my hands.

Feel the ground underneath your feet. What sensations do you notice?

The ground is slightly bouncy from the wood chips and gives a little because of the wet earth.

Bring to awareness what you see, what you hear, the sensations on your skin, the feeling of the ground underneath your feet. How do you feel?

Calm, relaxed and still.

If there was a word that decribes how this place makes you feel, what would that word be?

Safe.

**Repeat your word in your mind while you remain in your safe place.
What do you notice?**

A relaxed, tingling feeling in my body.

What do you notice happening in your body while you are in your safe place?

Feeling clam and a little sleepy.

Safe place exercise – Page 1

Think of a place where you can go on your own. Ideally a place not connected with friends or relatives. An outdoor place where you feel safe and relaxed. Write down a brief description of your place below.

Look ahead and notice the details of what you see. Write down what you see here. In particular, notice the details of what you see.

Look to your left and write down what you see. In particular notice the details of what you see.

Look to your right and write down what you see. In particular notice the details of what you see.

Listen to the sounds that you hear. What do you notice?

How do you feel when you hear these sounds?

Breathe in. What sensations to you notice in terms of how your breath feels? What does this place smell like?

Safe place exercise – Page 2

Become aware of the air against your skin. What tells you from what you feel on your skin that you are in this place?

Feel the ground underneath your feet. What sensations do you notice?

Bring to awareness what you see, what you hear, the sensations on your skin, the feeling of the ground underneath your feet. How do you feel?

If there was a word that decribes how this place makes you feel, what would that word be?

Repeat your word in your mind while you remain in your safe place.
What do you notice?

What do you notice happening in your body while you are in your safe place?

Time Date	Trigger	Behaviour	Consequences of behaviour	New behaviour	Consequences of new behaviour	Reflection

Chapter 14 Changing behaviour

A general idea behind behaviour change diaries is to bring problematic behaviour into conscious awareness. The majority of our behaviours occur automatically, and are governed by processes that occur outside of our conscious awareness.

Bringing problematic behaviours into conscious awareness is the first part of a change process. The second part of a change process is deciding to change, and then giving yourself alternative behaviour to replace the old one.

Behaviour change diary

Time: Date:	Trigger	Behaviour	Consequences of Behaviour	New behaviour	Consequences of new behaviour	Reflection

Behaviour change diary

Time: Date:	Trigger	Behaviour	Consequences of Behaviour	New behaviour	Consequences of new behaviour	Reflection
1.30pm, 14th July	Bump into someone on the street I have fallen out with.	Ignore them or keep conversation short.	Relationship with that person continues to be frosty and it creates bad feeling.	Talk with the other person in a civil manner. Be polite.	Relationship is more amicable and I don't feel bad or guilty.	It is better to say what needs to be said at the time and then put the problem behind me. The problem does not fester and I will have more amicable relationships.

Behaviour change diary

Time: Date:	Trigger	Behaviour	Consequences of Behaviour	New behaviour	Consequences of new behaviour	Reflection

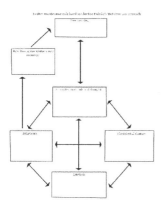

Chapter 15 Positive CBT cycles

Although generic CBT cycles are mostly used with negative automatic thoughts (NATs) it is often useful after completing a thought challenging record to place your new information into a positive cycle. To start this process off, write your new more balanced thought in the balanced thought box, and ask yourself what this thought might mean about you if it were true, or if you were to choose to believe it.

Repeat the new more balanced thought in your mind and scan your body. Notice any changes in your body's reaction when you hold that thought in mind. Reflect on what emotion you might be experiencing, and how thinking and feeling this way may influence your behaviour. Place all of this information into a positive generic cycle.

The positive generic CBT model

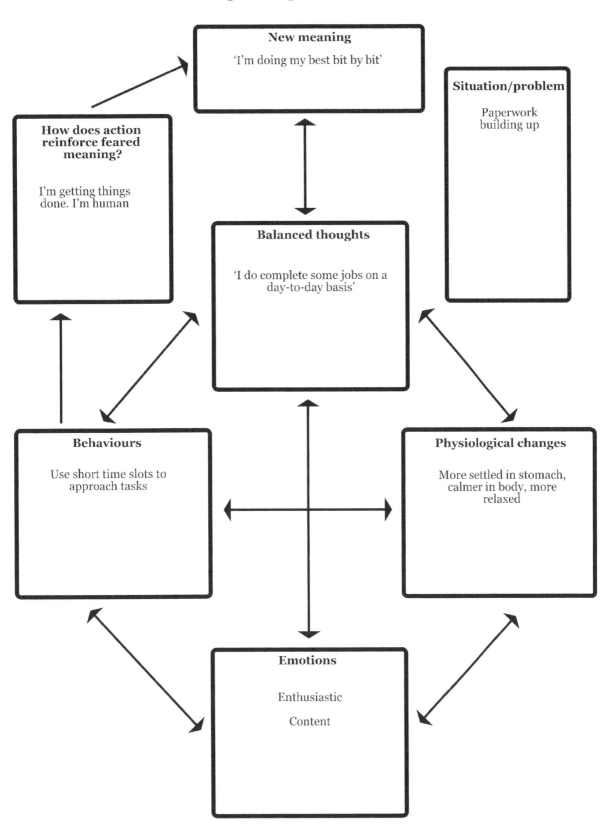

New meaning

'I'm doing my best bit by bit'

Situation/problem

Paperwork building up

How does action reinforce feared meaning?

I'm getting things done. I'm human

Balanced thoughts

'I do complete some jobs on a day-to-day basis'

Behaviours

Use short time slots to approach tasks

Physiological changes

More settled in stomach, calmer in body, more relaxed

Emotions

Enthusiastic

Content

The positive generic CBT model

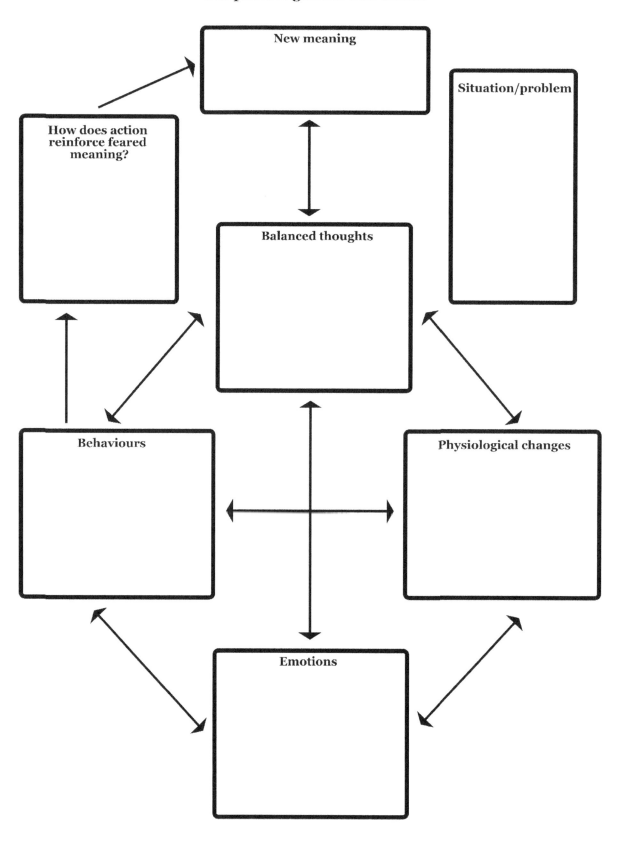

The positive generic CBT model

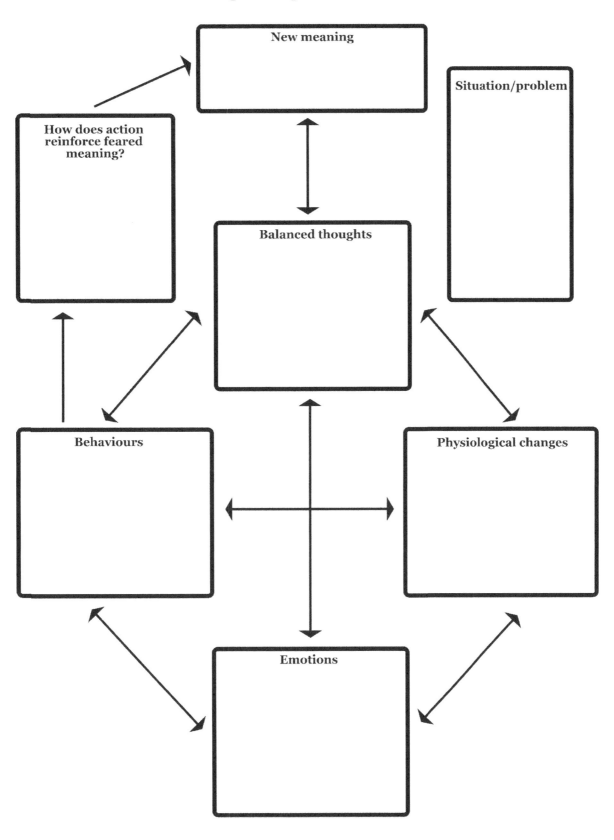

The positive generic CBT model

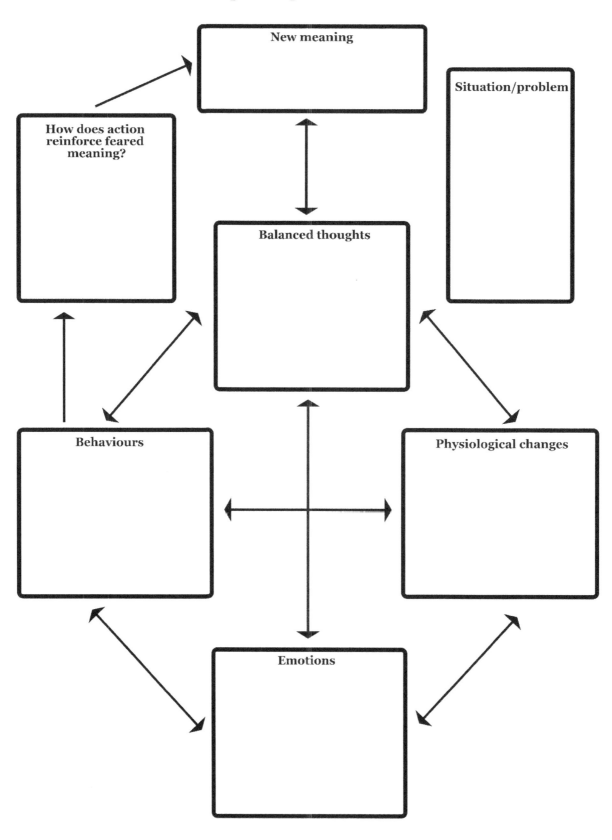

The positive generic CBT model

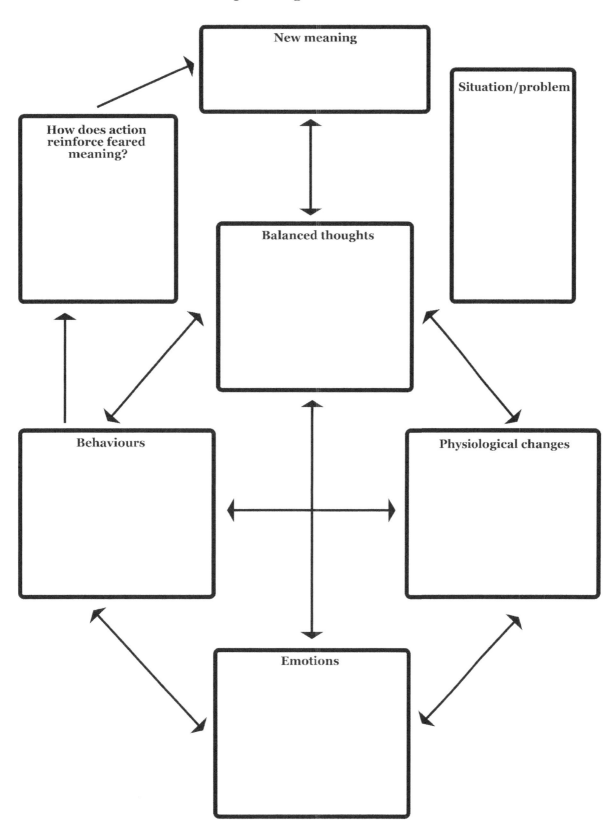

The positive generic CBT model

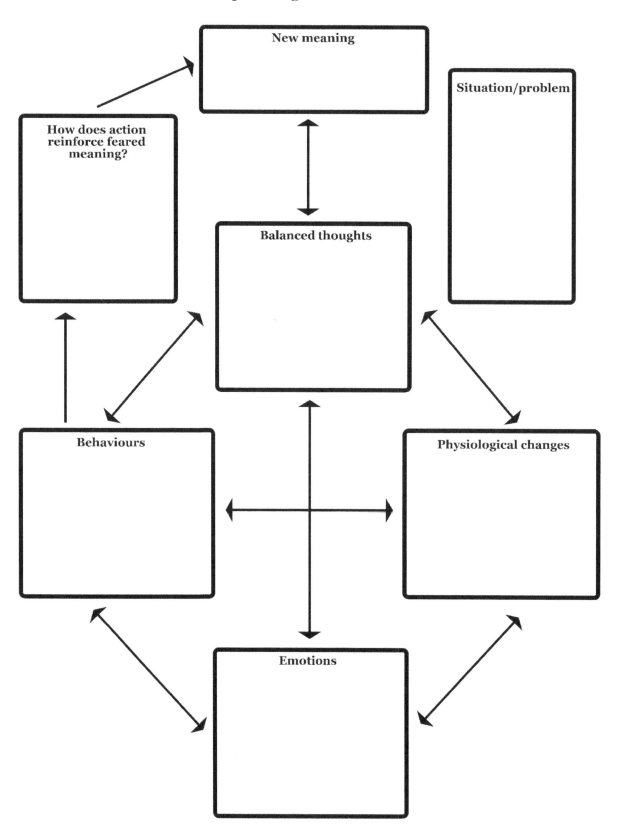

Behaviour goals sheet	
Old behaviour	New behaviour

Chapter 16 Behaviour goals

Once you have worked on a psychological explanation of your problems with your therapist you will have an idea about the types of behaviours that are keeping your problems in place. Much of the time safety behaviours need to be challenged to create lasting change. With most safety behaviours there is an alternative more adaptive behaviour that you could carry out instead. I have given some examples on the following page.

Behaviour goals sheet

Old behaviour	New behaviour
Drink alcohol to relax	Find other ways to relax; for example yoga, massage, exercise
Worry	Use problem-solving exercises rather than worry
Avoid conflict	Approach difficulties as quickly as possible using assertiveness
Over-estimate earnings	Under-estimate earnings
Avoid exercise	Build in exercise as part of a weekly routine
Ruminate over difficulties	Use mindfulness exercises
Procrastinate	Complete tasks that require a short time immediately
Work very long hours	Limit work hours
Take on too much responsibility	Share responsibility. Use pie exercise more often.
Eat chocolate at night as a reward	Use healthy rewards
Neglect self	Build healthy habits

Behaviour goals sheet

Old behaviour	New behaviour

Behaviour goals sheet

Old behaviour	New behaviour

Chapter 17 Systematic desensitisation

Perhaps the most effective way to approach feared situations or behaviours is to use a process known as systematic desensitisation. To complete systematic desensitisation you will need to write down a list of a) the things that you have been avoiding and b) behaviours that you fear carrying out. This list can be created in discussion with your therapist. Look at each item on your list and rate each item in terms of how much anxiety each item makes you feel.

To complete a systematic desensitisation process you will need to start with the least anxiety provoking item. Using the exposure worksheet in this chapter carry out the lowest anxiety provoking item until your anxiety reduces to zero or until your anxiety stabilises and you can easily tolerate your anxious feelings. It is important when you are carrying out systematic desensitisation that you **do not** move onto higher anxiety evoking items until you can easily tolerate lower anxiety evoking items. It is highly beneficial and good practice to repeat behaviours even when they feel mundane and/or boring.

Systematic desensitisation sheet

Feared situation or feared behaviour	What do I fear might happen?	Anxiety Rate out of 10 where 10 is the maximum
Reduce lecture preparation time to the same as other academics.	People will find out that I am not really up to the job and that I am a fraud.	9
Speak without thinking through exactly what I am going to say.	I will say something stupid and embarrass myself.	8
Focus on others instead of myself.	Dropping my guard will end up with me saying something stupid.	4
Allow my anxiety to be there.	My anxiety might take me by surprise and others might notice.	2
Say what I think a bit more in social situations.	People might judge me or think that I am stupid.	6
Stand in the foreground in social situations.	I will draw more attention to myself and will look awkward and uncomfortable.	5
Arrive early to social events.	I will feel uncomfortable and awkward and will have to make conversation with people .	5
Suspend worrying. Deal with things when and if they happen.	I will be unprepared and will flounder	5

Systematic desensitisation sheet

Feared situation or feared behaviour	What do I fear might happen?	Anxiety Rate out of 10 where 10 is the maximum

Systematic desensitisation sheet

Overall target situation, object or behaviour for desensitisation
Travelling on a tube

Individual area for desensitisation	Predicted distress level 0 to 10
Go into foyer of tube station. Stay there until distress reduces to zero and then exit tube station	2
Go down long escalator and back up to surface again	3
Use lift	6
Go on overland train accompanied by someone	7
Go on overland train alone	8
Go on tube accompanied by therapist	8
Go on tube accompanied by friend	9
Go on tube alone	10

Systematic desensitisation sheet

Overall target situation, object or behaviour for desensitisation

Use lift (part of desensitisation process of going on a tube)

Individual area for desensitisation	Predicted distress level 0 to 10
Go to lift (not used much) with therapist	1
Go in lift with doors open and get out again (with therapist)	2
Go in lift with doors open and get out again (without therapist)	3
Go in lift, let doors close and open and get out again (with therapist)	4
Go in lift let doors close and open and get out again (without therapist)	5
Go in lift let doors close and open, go down or up one floor and get out again (with therapist)	5
Go in lift let doors close and open, go down or up one floor and get out again (without therapist)	6
Go in lift let doors close and open, go down or up two floors and get out again (without therapist)	6

Systematic desensitisation sheet

Overall target situation, object or behaviour for desensitisation

Individual area for desensitisation	Predicted distress level 0 to 10

Exposure sheet

Exposure involves a) staying in a particular situation or b) continuing to use a particular behaviour until the situation or behaviour is very easy to tolerate. To help yourself reduce your anxiety in the longer term, assess your anxiety level before, during and after the situation you place yourself in or while you are using a new behaviour. After you have completed your exposure work think to yourself about what you have learnt from your experience. This will further embed your experiential learning (learning by doing/experiencing).

Exposure sheet

Time: Date:	Situation	Anxiety before (0 to 10 where 10 is max)	Anxiety during (0 to 10 where 10 is max)	Anxiety after (0 to 10 where 10 is max)	What did I learn?
7 pm 17 Jan	Staying with and welcoming anxiety during a social event	6	2	2	Staying with and welcoming anxiety during a social event

Exposure sheet

Time: Date:	Situation	Anxiety before (0 to 10 where 10 is max)	Anxiety during (0 to 10 where 10 is max)	Anxiety after (0 to 10 where 10 is max)	What did I learn?

Exposure sheet

Time: Date:	Situation	Anxiety before (0 to 10 where 10 is max)	Anxiety during (0 to 10 where 10 is max)	Anxiety after (0 to 10 where 10 is max)	What did I learn?

Exposure sheet

Time: Date:	Situation	Anxiety before (0 to 10 where 10 is max)	Anxiety during (0 to 10 where 10 is max)	Anxiety after (0 to 10 where 10 is max)	What did I learn?

Exposure sheet

Time: Date:	Situation	Anxiety before (0 to 10 where 10 is max)	Anxiety during (0 to 10 where 10 is max)	Anxiety after (0 to 10 where 10 is max)	What did I learn?

Memory aids

Thinking biases

Thinking biases can create huge distortions in your thinking and can affect the way that you process information. Having a sheet of thinking biases handy can be especially useful when challenging NATs.

Brain organisation

Understanding the basics of how the brain operates can be very useful when completing CBT. You can find out a lot more about how the brain works by reading our other books or books from our reference list at the back of this book.

Feelings/focussing exercise

This exercise is designed to help you access your feelings on a more regular basis. Without accessing your feelings, it is very difficult to create changes using CBT.

Rumination and worry handout

Prior to learning about it in therapy most people do not realise how much impact rumination and worry has on the neuro-biology of the brain and how it can maintain symptoms. Hopefully as soon as you recognise that you are ruminating or worrying you will have more choice about how you decide to react.

Safety behaviour sheets and potential behavioural experiments

I have made a list of specific problems and common safety behaviours. I have also made suggestions about potential behavioural experiments you could use to challenge your safety behaviours.

Memory aid 1 Thinking biases and cognitive distortions

Within CBT a view is built on a premise that what we think can affect the way in which we view the world, the way that we feel, and the way that we behave. Much of the time when we feel emotionally distressed, our minds distort the way that we process information. In CBT we call these processes **cognitive distortions**. Cognitive distortions are changes in our mental perception that can give us a skewed view of the world.

When we experience cognitive distortions our thinking style can move from being balanced, flexible, expansive, and considering to a more rigid style, not dissimilar to what you might expect from small children. Such cognitive processes (whether verbal or image based) encourage us to think that we can see the future, or make life events feel much bigger or smaller than they really are. A list of the most common thought distortions has been placed on the next page.

Thinking bias	What to look out for
All or nothing thinking	Viewing things as either right or wrong. There is no middle ground. Things are either perfect or fundamentally flawed. There is just black or white; grey does not exist: e.g., always/never, good/bad.
Disqualifying the positive	Positives don't count; there is nothing special about the way I did it: e.g., 'That only happened because I was lucky.'
Emotional reasoning	Using emotions as evidence: e.g., 'I feel it, so it must be true.'
Fortune telling	Predicting the future in a negative way without any real evidence: e.g., 'It's going to be terrible.'; 'It will be a disaster'; 'I just know it'.
Mind reading	Drawing conclusions about what others are thinking without any evidence: e.g., 'She doesn't like me.'; 'They think I am stupid.'
Mental filtering	Selecting specific negative ideas to dwell on and ignoring all of the positive ones.
Shoulds, oughts and musts	Having ideas that things can only be done one way. 'People should ...'; 'I must ...'; 'I really ought to ...'; 'He shouldn't have ...''
Personalising	Focusing on things in the immediate environment and connecting it to the self. Thinking, for example, 'she did that deliberately because she knew that I wouldn't like that!' The world revolves around the self.
Over-generalising	Taking single events or circumstances and viewing them as happening more often than they really do. Thinking that things happen everywhere.
Magnification or minimisation	Taking events and distorting them. Not dissimilar to looking at one's self through a fairground distorting mirror. Making things bigger or smaller than they really are.

Memory aid 2 Brain organisation visual version

BIG JIM: There are three parts to the brain that you will find out about when you do CBT. The clever part is based at the top of the brain.

The clever part is better at doing difficult things like crosswords, mathematics and solving problems.

At the bottom of the brain is the animal part.

The animal part is very loyal, a bit like my dog, but is also pretty stupid and believes everything that you tell it. It is in charge of feelings so we need to be careful with it.

There is another little part in between the clever part and the animal part. It sorts out problems between the two of them. This part is the 'minder'.

The minder helps the brainy part sort out the animal when it gets a bit upset or angry. The minder is very good at calming down the animal part and can manage it, if it gets upset.

Overall the brain is a bit like this picture below.

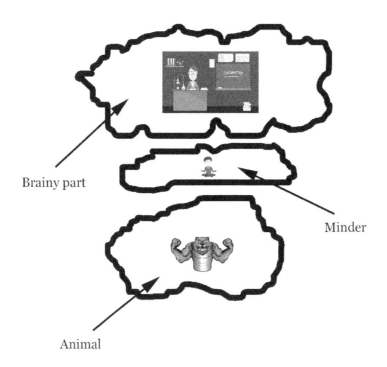

Brainy part

Minder

Animal

SALLY: Professor Nut. Do you have anything to add about what people might find out about the brain?

PROFESSOR NUT: Have a look at my diagram overleaf. If you look at the brain from the top down everything that you can see on the surface is called the **neo-cortex**. The neo-cortex is a part of the brain that we use to think, plan and solve complex problems. You will need to use this part of the brain quite a bit when you do CBT. The lower areas of the brain that reside underneath the neo-cortex are known by people in my field as **sub-cortical regions**. The sub-cortical regions could be described as the primitive or animal brain, as we share similar brain structures with mammals. This part of the brain is mainly interested in survival. The sub-cortical region is where our emotional reactions come from.

The sub-cortical regions contain an area of the brain known as the limbic system. The limbic system and the area beneath it are where emotions are generated. The amygdala, which is located on both sides of the brain, in particular triggers emotions such as anxiety.

The part of the brain that Big Jim calls 'the minder' is technically known as the **pre-frontal cortex**. The pre-frontal cortex is an extremely important part of the brain in terms of human evolution. It acts as a messenger between the neo-cortex and the primitive brain regions that lie beneath it.

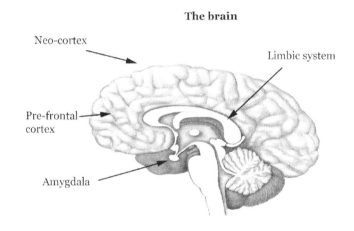

The brain

Neo-cortex

Limbic system

Pre-frontal cortex

Amygdala

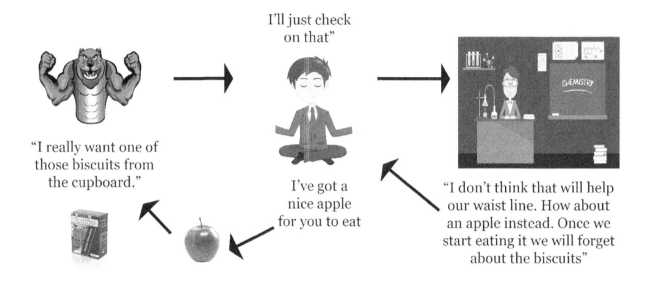

The pre-frontal cortex sits on top of the limbic system and acts as a communication system between the neo-cortex and the sub-cortical region. It has many important jobs. It quietens down noise in the mind and it can call off emotional reactions created by sub-cortical regions. We also use this part of our brain to think about our thinking. I've just added a few notes to Big Jim's picture and put it on the right.

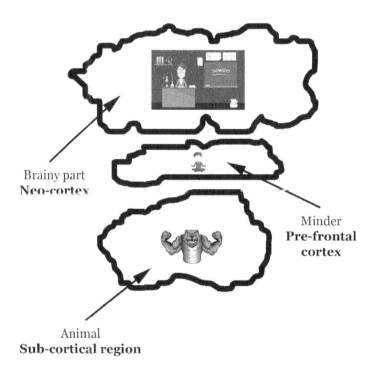

154

Memory aid 3
Brain
organisation

Neo-cortex

This is a part of the brain responsible for thinking, planning, and logical thought.

Pre-frontal cortex

The pre-frontal cortex is an essential part of the brain for psychological wellness. It often becomes compromised in people with mental health problems. The pre-frontal cortex sits on top of the limbic system acting as a communication system between the neo-cortex and the sub-cortical region. It has many important jobs. It quietens down 'noise' in the mind and it can call off emotional reactions created by sub-cortical regions. We also use this part of our brain to think about our thinking.

The pre-frontal cortex becomes temporarily impaired in people with anxiety disorders and can often lead to individuals with anxiety feeling that they are unable to think straight. In depression the pre-frontal cortex can become impaired for longer periods, contributing to poor concentration and difficulties with attention.

The limbic system

The limbic system is based in the middle of brain within the **sub-cortical regions.** The sub-cortical regions (which take their name because they are located underneath the brains cortex area) could be described as the primitive or animal brain, as we share similar brain structures with mammals. The sub-cortical regions predominant interest is in survival and this is where our emotional reactions come from.

The limbic system and the areas beneath it are where emotions are generated. The amygdala, which is located on both sides of the brain, in particular triggers emotions such as anxiety.

The brain

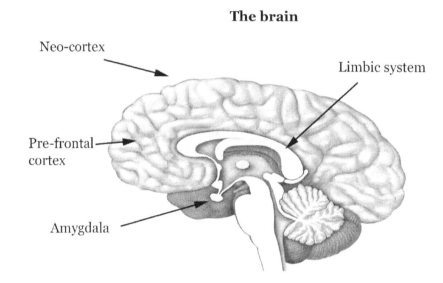

Neo-cortex

Limbic system

Pre-frontal cortex

Amygdala

Memory aid 4 Emotions exercise

- Begin by noticing where you feel your emotion most strongly.

- Keep your focus on your feeling. Place your hand wherever you feel your emotion more strongly. You are placing your hand on your body where your emotion is, because many of us who are prone to avoiding emotions unconsciously and automatically move away from feeling emotions, and go into our heads instead. You are gaining a connection with your emotions and keeping your focus on how you are feeling. Placing your hand on the part of your body where you feel your anxiety more strongly will also act as a reminder to you, to keep your focus on your emotions. It is very important while you are doing this exercise to focus on feeling your feelings and remind yourself that you really are willing for your emotions to be there.

- Focussing on the part of your body underneath your hand with your mind, examine exactly what your emotion feels like. For example, how much space do your feelings take up? How painful or uncomfortable are your feelings? Rate the intensity of your feeling between 1 and 10, where 10 is the highest level of intensity. While you continue to feel your feelings, mentally give your feelings permission to take up the space that they are taking up in your body. If you want to take things a little further you could also speak to your distress. Internally, try saying something along the lines of 'Thank you for being there' … "There are very good reasons for you being there. Bear in mind the idea that, from the primitive minds point of view there is a good reason for your anxiety being there, even if it does not make sense logically. Follow that by saying 'You are welcome to stay there for as long as you want.'

- Bear in mind from the sub-cortical region's (primitive mind's) point of view that if it notices during its screening process that there is a cue to a potential threat, which may be physical or psychological, it is just doing its job properly if it brings the threat to your attention and helps you to prepare. The threat does not need to be logical, real or valid in the current time mode. If it has been perceived as a threat in the past, or you have previously confirmed the existence of the threat by withdrawing from this threat in the past, then from the primitive mind's point of view the threat is still active.

- While feeling your symptoms of anxiety it is important when you speak to your feelings that you really mean what you are saying. Let go of all your thoughts and focus on your feeling. The importance of your self-communication is not in the words that you use but rather your intention behind your words. Keep an idea in mind of accepting, recognising, being grateful and being patient. Do this for a minute or so and bring your awareness to what happens.

- Stay with your emotions as the intensity gradually decreases.

- It is important in the early stages of CBT when you are experiencing anxiety, low mood, guilt and anger to practise being with your feelings as much as possible. This will help you in two ways. First, it will help you to fear your feelings less; second it will make it more likely that you will be able to use this acceptance approach when you are experiencing higher levels of distress.

- Bear in mind that in a state of heightened distress the frontal lobes – where most of our logical thinking occurs – stop working somewhat. Doing the same thing over and over again when you are not so distressed will make it more likely that you will be able to access and use this approach automatically when you really need it.

Memory aid 5 Rumination and worry

CBT THERAPIST: Most people who experience mental health problems will spend a significant portion of their time ruminating or worrying. Because these processes tend to maintain emotional difficulties, it is not uncommon for them to be discussed in CBT sessions.

Rumination is a process of churning negative thoughts over in one's mind. Most ruminative thoughts are connected to the self and the past. Some people suggest that rumination is useful because it can help to create lots of possibilities, and can offer solutions when we are faced with specific problems. Rumination, however, does not work well when we try to analyse our way out of low mood.

A process of rumination is kept in place by the questions we ask ourselves. For example, we might ask, 'Why does this keep happening to me?' or 'What's wrong with me?' The questions that we ask ourselves throw up answers that, in turn, can lead us to ask more questions. Before long, if this process continues unstopped, we can end up confirming our worst fears; for example, that we are worthless, wrong, useless, bad and such like. The irony of the process is that in our search for ways to avoid current or future painful feelings by ruminating, we end up dwelling on the past, and we can end up feeling worse than ever. It's not dissimilar to using a shovel to dig ourselves out of a hole. The more we dig, the deeper the hole gets! The problem is that often we do not feel that we have any other way of solving our problems, so we continue to use the same strategy, even though we know it does not work.

CLIENT: So how is worry similar or different to ruminating?

CBT THERAPIST: Worry is similar to ruminating in that it is also a process of thought churning. The main difference is that worry is focused on the future and being able to cope with potential outcomes.

When people worry, they think about upcoming situations and ask questions such as: 'What will I do if this happens?' 'What is the worst thing that could happen?' or 'What if this happens?' They do this because they think that if they can imagine the worst-case scenario, then they will be able to put things in place to deal with whatever happens in a particular situation. They think if they can work out what might happen in advance then they will be safe. Ironically, however, just like rumination, in an attempt to achieve certainty and to feel safe, we can end up feeling more frightened than ever, and also experience frightening intrusive thoughts.

CLIENT: Intrusive thoughts?

CBT THERAPIST: An intrusive thought is a thought that pushes its way into awareness with extreme urgency. Intrusive thoughts often appear to come out of nowhere and carry high levels of emotional distress with them. Ironically, intrusive thoughts alone can trigger heightened anxiety.

Before I explain why intrusive thoughts may occur, I want to offer a simple analogy about the functioning of the mind for our readers.

First, I'd like our readers to recognise that they have a **conscious mind**. When people use their conscious minds they are awake to thoughts, images or sensations that they experience. I'd like us to imagine that the conscious mind is a bit like a magic white board that begins to erase what is written on it after only a few seconds. Because the ink or information expressed using the ink disappears so rapidly the only way to keep anything live on this white board is to continuously write on it over and over again. When new information is written on the white board, information that was on the white board previously disappears even more rapidly. A further point to note is that the amount of information that can be written on the whiteboard at any one point in time is limited due to the whiteboard's small size.

CLIENT: So you're saying the mind is like a whiteboard? I'm not sure I understand.

CBT THERAPIST: Do you mind if I demonstrate with you? It's much easier to show our readers how this works rather than to explain it. Before we start, I just want to let you know that this is not a test. It's just a little exercise so that you can find out how much information your mind can hold onto. I am going to start by asking you to remember five random numbers and letters. Are you ready?

CLIENT: Yes.

CBT THERAPIST: 5A3KQ. Have you got that?

CLIENT: Yes. I think so!

CBT THERAPIST: Alright. I now want you to remember these numbers as well. 27KR1. Right, can you repeat that sequence for me?

CLIENT: 27KR1.

CBT THERAPIST: Good. And, the first sequence?

CLIENT: Erm... [a big pause follows] ... 57 ... Q... It seems to have gone out of my head... I'm sorry.

CBT THERAPIST: There's no need to be sorry. This is exactly what is meant to happen. This is how the mind works. We just gave your internal whiteboard an impossible task. Hardly anyone can recall more than nine randomly presented units of information unless they use specialised memory techniques, and I just gave you ten. That's why I'm saying the whiteboard is small in size.

I'll explain it a bit more. A benefit of the whiteboard's disappearing ink process is that it is constantly available for continuous use. As a result of this, huge amounts of information can be written on the whiteboard during the period of its lifetime. In many respects, it could be suggested that we could feel grateful that the whiteboard loses access to information so quickly. If it didn't, it would quite quickly become jammed up with too much information and become unusable.

Taking this idea further, I'd like us to imagine that our **out-of-conscious processes** work a little bit like a building that the whiteboard is housed in. For our readers' benefit, I'll just explain that out-of-conscious processes are brain functions that we are unaware of, or mental processes that go on in the back of our minds.

CLIENT: And what's the significance of associating the out-of-conscious mind with a building?

CBT THERAPIST: I'm saying that out-of-conscious processes are like a building because the amount of brain space required for out-of-conscious thinking is absolutely huge in comparison to the amount of brain space used for the white board. The building is also three-dimensional, unlike the two-dimensional whiteboard, and there are also multiple rooms and secret passageways.

CLIENT: I understand why it is big, but what does the three-dimensional layout of the building represent, with multiple rooms and such like?

CBT THERAPIST: This represents an idea that the out-of-conscious mind can think on several different levels at the same time. It can absorb information from our environment, take care of all of our bodily functions, plan our activities, assist our communication, and think about problems we have in our lives without us being aware of it. It can also use symbols, images and words to create ideas and connect them up in a way that we would struggle to do consciously. What it can do is really quite incredible! In this building there are also filing cabinets crammed with information that we thought we had forgotten about, and there are reams of papers lying around waiting to be filed.

CLIENT: What do the reams of papers represent?

CBT THERAPIST: The reams of paper represent thoughts that we have not fully processed or ideas that we are currently working on. Many people may have several hundred or even thousands of different thought strands they are working on at any one time. Thought strands may be about relationships with different people, hobbies or interests, work projects, holidays and such like. Information does not disappear easily from this building but very often it can get lost or misfiled.

CLIENT: So how does it get lost or misfiled?

CBT THERAPIST: There is so much information in this building or in people's minds that sometimes it is hard for them to find what they are looking for. The more information that's in the building the harder it is to find what they need.

Now imagine that in this building there is a little librarian who is very loyal to you and will try to find answers to anything that you ask using the whiteboard, even if it means working through the night. Sometimes the librarian finds information quickly, sometimes it might take days, but when the librarian finds answers to questions posed on the whiteboard it will post it an answer on the whiteboard just as soon as space becomes available.

CLIENT: I'm still not sure I fully understand this analogy of a librarian. How does this work with real problems?

CBT THERAPIST: OK. Let's imagine that you are walking down the street one day and on the other side there is a girl whose face you recognise. You are immediately aware that you know her but this is not where you usually see her. You ask yourself 'Where do I know her from?' a few times. Nothing comes to mind immediately and you carry on doing whatever you were doing before. You may even forget that you asked that question as it disappears from your conscious awareness and is replaced by other things. However, a little while later, maybe a few hours, days, or sometimes weeks later, an idea pops into your mind telling you where you knew the person you saw in the street from. How do you think this might happen?

CLIENT: Well, I guess the little librarian had not forgotten that I had asked that question. Perhaps she was going through the filing cabinets looking for an answer or maybe she waited for me to go somewhere and suddenly remembered.

CBT THERAPIST: That's what I'm saying. As soon as an opportunity occurred and there was space available on the whiteboard, the librarian posted the information. A useful rule of thumb, therefore, will be to assume that when we ask our brain a question it will continue to work on questions posed to it even though we may have consciously forgotten that we have asked the questions in the first place. Usually the little librarian will put thoughts or information in a queue to enter conscious awareness. In this respect, answers to questions you have asked will wait patiently to pop into your mind when there is space available or when the mind is not occupied with something else.

CLIENT: Is that why so many thoughts go through my head at night just as I want to go to sleep?

CBT THERAPIST: Yes, that what I'm getting at. You will have access to these thoughts at night because your mind is not focused on other things.

CLIENT: What about the other thoughts you mentioned earlier? I think you said they were intrusive thoughts. I used to get those a lot.

CBT THERAPIST: Intrusive thoughts are different to the above-mentioned patient-type of thoughts that we have. They are not dissimilar to the librarian pushing through a registered letter for your attention. Intrusive thoughts are pushed through to consciousness as a priority, pushing out any other information that is currently on line. You may be talking with someone when one of these thoughts pops into your head. For example, if you are socially anxious, an image of yourself looking odd could suddenly be pushed into your mind. Intrusive thoughts are sent with high degrees of importance and you will notice them as a result of the emotional intensity that comes with them.

CLIENT: So where do they come from?

CBT THERAPIST: There may be many factors responsible for the creation of intrusive thoughts. One way in which they may be generated is by worrying or asking 'What if?' questions. This type of questioning process certainly appears to increase the likelihood of intrusive thoughts being pushed into consciousness. It is important to recognise that when we receive intrusive thought messages they are not 'evidence' for anything. Although intrusive thoughts often feel uncomfortable, because they bring fear with them, it does not make these thoughts any more real than any other thoughts that pop into your mind.

I think the best way to explain this is by talking about a young man I worked with a little while ago. Gregory was a big worrier. He would often go through a process of worry, asking 'What if?' questions to his mind and his brain would usually send him back the worst possible things that could happen, or what could go wrong. His intentions for worrying were positive, as he felt that this type of questioning process could keep him safe. He thought that if he knew about the types of problems that might occur in advance then he could be prepared for them. Before going to the cinema with friends Gregory would ask himself about what could go wrong. His obedient mind usually sent him answers. One type of answer generated and sent to his conscious awareness was that he might end up in a middle seat feeling panicky, with everyone around noticing him, and he would feel humiliated.

CLIENT: I think most people would be anxious about that, wouldn't they?

CBT THERAPIST: They might do if they worried a lot about what people thought about them. But remember, nothing had *actually* happened at this point. This was all in his mind. But, based on the ideas that his mind gave him, Gregory decided to take action and sit at the back near an aisle seat so that he could make a quick exit if required. Gregory then began to think of how he could position himself in an aisle seat. He thought that if he could go in first in his group of friends he could stand near an aisle seat and gesture to others to go in ahead of him. His mind came up with a further idea, such as if anyone questioned his need to sit in an aisle seat, he would say that he had a stomach ache and might need to go to the bathroom. He also had thoughts about phoning his friends up at the last minute and telling them that he couldn't make it. The amount of worrying that Gregory experienced before going to the cinema made the whole process of going to the cinema a difficult experience rather than the enjoyable experience that it could have been. Gregory's mind also reminded him how strange he was for engaging in this type of behaviour, and his friends would never think that he was like that.

CLIENT: So what happened to him?

CBT THERAPIST: A big risk for Gregory was deciding not to ask 'What if?' questions. A big part of Gregory thought that asking himself these questions kept him prepared, safe and not vulnerable. Recognising that all thoughts that come into awareness are simply offerings sent by the mind and not ideas supported by evidence made a significant difference to Gregory. Gregory learnt how to stand back and observe his thoughts, and recognise that any thought that came into awareness was just a suggestion. Just because he had a thought did not mean it needed to be dealt with. As such, learning to notice his thoughts made a significant difference to him.

Many people's minds come up with all sorts of negative ideas when they worry. In Gregory's case, a worry for him was losing control, being thought of by others as weak, and others thinking that there was something wrong with him. I drew a diagram on my office whiteboard for Gregory to look at. I have copied this onto the next page. It's the same diagram that I mentioned earlier the generic CBT cycle.

The generic CBT cycle can be very useful to us here to explain what was happening to Gregory. Gregory engaged in numerous avoidant-type behaviours that tended to confirm his fear-based thoughts still further. By carrying out avoidant behaviours Gregory did not collect alternative evidence that challenged his fears.

CBT THERAPIST: The example on the next page shows how the interactions between thoughts, feelings and behaviour have a tendency to maintain problems. In this case, interfering with Gregory's worry processes led to him having less frightening thoughts, which in turn led to a reduction in his tendency to want to avoid situations.

Gregory's example

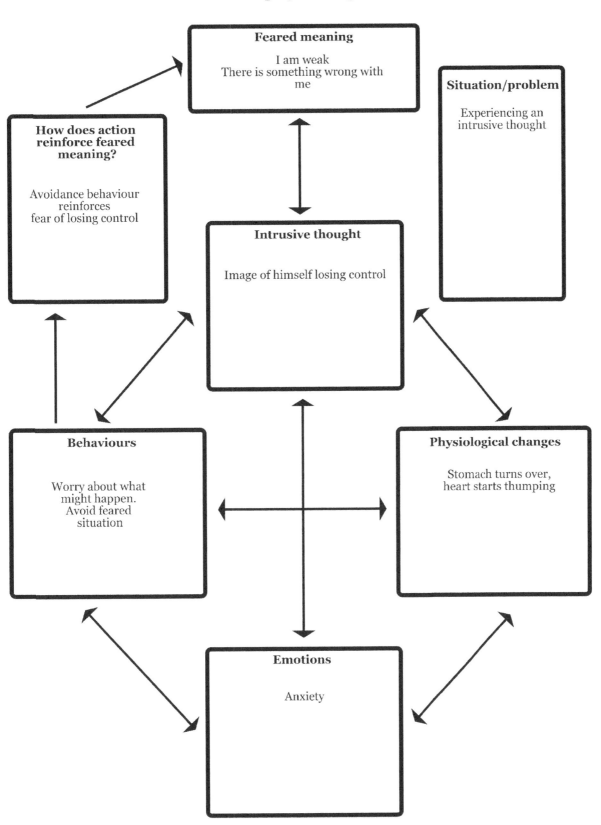

Feared meaning

I am weak
There is something wrong with me

Situation/problem

Experiencing an intrusive thought

How does action reinforce feared meaning?

Avoidance behaviour reinforces
fear of losing control

Intrusive thought

Image of himself losing control

Behaviours

Worry about what might happen.
Avoid feared situation

Physiological changes

Stomach turns over, heart starts thumping

Emotions

Anxiety

Appendix

Examples of safety behaviour in depression

- Say "Yes" to all requests
- Look for approval from others
- Compare self with others
- Withdraw emotionally
- Hide feelings
- Keep conversations short
- Turn down invitations
- Avoid confrontation
- Use drugs or alcohol to cope
- Ignore feelings
- Drop activities if not 100%
- Avoid conversations about emotions

Examples of safety behaviour in social anxiety

- Use diazepam or beta-blockers before social events e.g., business meetings.
- Carry a supply of diazepam just in case.
- Drink alcohol before going out to relax.
- Avoid situations where social anxiety has occurred in the past or where it may occur in the future.
- Go to the toilet before going out (related to fear of using lavatories and others overhearing lavatory use.)
- Have someone with you when going to social situations.
- Carry a bottle of water to help with a dry mouth.
- Sit close to an exit so as to escape unnoticed.
- Hold onto or lean onto something supportive to hide shaking or trembling.
- Wear light clothing, fan self or stand near a window or a doorway to prevent over-heating. Alternatively wear more clothes to conceal sweating.
- Have tissue ready to wipe hands to conceal sweaty hands.
- Use heavy makeup to avoid others noticing blushing or cover face with hair.
- Drink out a bottle rather than a glass to avoid others noticing shaking hands.
- Have stories ready to put on an act of social competence and to have something interesting to say.
- Focus on self to assess social performance.
- Avoid conversations with people.
- Stand in a corner to keep a low profile.
- Keep conversations as short as possible to avoid revealing anything that could be self-incriminating.
- Focus on appearance.
- Try to control facial expressions.
- Avoid eye-contact with others.
- Mentally rehearse what is being said before it is said.
- Have excuses about a need to leave pre-planned and ready.

Examples of safety behaviour in panic attacks

- Use diazepam, a drug that alters neurotransmitter functioning to produce a calming effect, or beta-blockers before certain situations, e.g., using public transport, business meetings etc.
- Carry a supply of diazepam just in case.
- Do not move too fast due to fear of heart rate increase.
- Drink alcohol before going out to relax.
- Avoid situations where a panic attack has occurred in the past or where one may occur in the future.
- Do not eat before going out if related to a fear of vomiting.
- Go to the toilet before going out if related to fear of losing control of bowels.
- Have someone with you when in potential situations where panic could occur.
- Sit in places near to an exit in public places.
- Hold onto or lean onto something supportive.
- Hold breath, keep an eye on emotions.
- Fan self to stop self over-heating.
- Distract self, for example watch television.
- Carry a brown paper bag to breath in and out of.
- Carry a bottle of water in case of dry mouth.
- Carry a plastic bag if related to fear of vomiting.

Examples of safety behaviour in health anxiety

- Monitor any unusual symptoms in body.
- Seek reassurance.
- Make an appointment with Doctor or alternatively avoid doctors completely.
- Go onto the internet to complete research.
- Complete on-line assessments to self-diagnose.
- Scan body.
- Complete exercises to check if body is working OK.
- Worry about ability to cope with various physical disorders.
- Request medical tests from doctor or alternatively avoid medical tests totally.
- Request medical checks to rule out disorders.
- Control diet.

Examples of safety behaviour in OCD

- Avoid situations or people that may trigger obsessional thoughts.
- Re-trace steps.
- Go back and check on things that you are unsure of.
- Complete ritualistic behaviour, such as touching wood to stop things from happening.
- Complete mental calculations, for example, the times tables to distract self from emotions.
- Push away intrusive thoughts.
- Complete activities a certain number of times.
- Perform activities in a particular order.
- Wear particular jewellery or make-up.
- Carry certain items.
- Check and re-check to make sure that you have not left anything behind.
- Look for reassurance from others.
- Stay with safe people.
- Clean things to avoid contamination.
- Hold onto items or hoard items.

Examples of safety behaviour in phobic anxiety and post-trauma

- Avoid certain objects or places. This may be related to something frightening that happened in the past.
- Avoid certain forms of transport.
- Take specific alternative safer routes when travelling.
- Avoid certain smells, sensations, tastes, physical feelings that produce anxiety.
- Ask for reassurance or ask others to check things for you.
- Go to places with safe people.
- Avoid watching television programs about certain subjects.
- Try to be in control of others when you feel in an unsafe situation. For example, giving advice to others on how to drive, what to be careful of and such like.

Potential behavioural experiments for social anxiety

Safety behaviour	New alternative behaviour
Drink alcohol before going out to relax.	Go to social events in a state of sobriety.
Go to the toilet before going out (related to fear of using lavatories and others overhearing lavatory use.) Not being able to urinate at a urinal.	Use a lavatory in a public building. Use the lavatory while others are there. If male urinate in a urinal while other men are there. If unable to urinate wait for as long as is necessary.
Have someone with you when going to social situations.	Go to a social event alone.
Carry a bottle of water (to help with a dry mouth).	Leave water at home. Let dry mouth be there.
Sit close to an exit, so as to escape unnoticed.	Sit in a central area where you will have to move past people to leave the situation.
Hold onto or lean onto something supportive to hide shaking or trembling.	Allow hands to tremble. Allow others to see. Use external focus to assess what actually happens.
Wear light clothing, fan self or stand near a window or a doorway to prevent over-heating. Alternatively, wear more clothes to conceal sweating.	Wear normal clothing and stand in a warmer part of the room. Use external focus to assess what actually happens.
Have tissue ready to wipe hands to conceal sweaty hands.	Shake hands with somebody without wiping your hands first with tissues.
Use heavy makeup to avoid others noticing blushing or cover face with hair.	Use less make-up. Give permission for self to blush. Allow blushing experience to come and go. Use external focus to assess what actually happens.
Drink out a bottle rather than a glass to avoid others noticing shaking hands.	Drink out of a glass. If hands shake give permission for this to occur. Focus externally to assess what actually happens.
Have stories ready to put on an act of social competence and to have something interesting to say.	Go through a social event without telling stories or offering an acting performance.

	Practice active listening instead, using external focus.
Focus on self to assess social performance.	Focus on others. Be really curious and interested about what others think and how they behave.
Avoid conversations with people.	Start a conversation with a new person. Introduce yourself to them, by telling them your name.
Stand in a corner to keep a low profile.	Stand in a more prominent position where you are likely to interact with more people.
Keep conversations as short as possible to avoid revealing anything that could be self-incriminating.	Offer up some information about yourself that you would not normally. Assess what others reactions are.
Focus on appearance.	Focus on what you like about other people's appearance.
Try to control facial expressions by focussing on face.	Focus externally and give permission for your face to do whatever it chooses.
Avoid eye-contact with others.	Increase eye contact with others.
Mentally rehearse what is being said before it is said.	Speak without thinking and assess what actually happens.
Have excuses about why you need to leave pre-planned and ready.	Go to events without any pre-planning.

Potential behavioural experiments for anxiety or panic attacks

Safety behaviour	New alternative behaviour
Carry a supply of supply of diazepam everywhere.	Leave diazepam in the car when you visit the shops.
Do not move too fast for fear of heart rate increase.	Increase heart rate using exercise and observe what actually happens.
Drink alcohol before going out to relax.	Drink alcohol after you go out.
Avoid situations where you have had panic attacks in the past.	Gradually approach situations where panic attacks have occurred before.
Do not eat before going out (if you have a fear of vomiting).	Eat a small meal before going out.
Go to the restroom before going out. If fear is related to loss of control of bowels.	Hold off going to the restroom before going out unless you really need to go.
Have a safe person with you.	Leave safe person for a little while and see how you cope.
Carry a brown paper bag to breath in and out of.	Leave brown paper bag at home.
Carry a bottle of water just in case of dry mouth.	Hydrate with water before you go out.
Carry a plastic bag if fear is related to vomiting.	Leave plastic bag at home for longer period.
Sit near to an exit.	Gradually sit further and further from an exit.
Hold onto or lean onto something supportive.	Trust your body's ability to balance without holding onto anything.
Hold breath.	Focus on breathing.
Monitor anxiety.	Focus externally.
Fan self to stop self over heating.	Give permission for body to heat up as much as it wants.
Distract self to avoid noticing emotion.	Focus on emotion, stay with it and take it with you.

Potential behavioural experiments for health anxiety

Safety behaviour	New alternative behaviour
Monitor any unusual symptoms in body.	Focus externally.
Seek reassurance from loved ones.	Hold off seeking reassurance.
Make an appointment with Doctor.	Limit appointments with doctor. Make appointment as far ahead as possible.
Go onto the internet to complete research.	Limit intent searched. Post phone internet searches.
Complete on-line health assessments to self-diagnose.	Watch television instead or read a book.
Worry about ability to cope with various disorders.	Decide to deal with eventualities if or when they happen.
Request repeated medical tests from doctor.	Limit tests to reasonable intervals discussed with your doctor.
Request medical tests to rule out disorders when there are no symptoms.	Wait for symptoms before requesting a medical test.

Potential behavioural experiments for OCD

Safety behaviour	New alternative behaviour
Avoid situations or people that may trigger obsessional thoughts.	Carry out daily activities. Do not avoid people or places that you come across.
Retrace steps.	Post phone retracing steps.
Go back and check things that you are unsure of.	If you have checked already once leave it.
Complete ritualistic behaviour, for example, touching wood.	Post ritualistic behaviour and wait for urge to die down.
Complete mental calculations in head to distract from emotions.	Put 100% attention onto feeling feelings.
Push away intrusive thoughts. If you believe that thinking about them will make them real.	Recognise intrusive thoughts. Allow them to come and go in their own time.
Complete activities a certain number of times.	Reduce the number of time that you complete activities.
Perform activities in a particular order.	Deliberately change the order.
Wear particular make-up or jewellery.	Change make-up or jewellery.
Carry certain items.	Leave items behind for gradually longer periods of time.
Check and re-check that you have not left anything behind.	Check once and go.
Look for reassurance for others.	Drop reassurance.
Encourage others to engage in checks or rituals.	If you need to complete a checking behaviour do it on your own. Ask relatives not to co-operate with completing obsessional behaviours.
Stay with safe people.	Spend time away from safe people.
Clean things to avoid contamination.	Reduce cleaning activity. Post-phone cleaning.
Hold on items or hoard things.	Gradually throw things that you don't need any more away. Thrown away a piece of unnecessary clutter at least once a day.

Potential behavioural experiments for phobic anxiety

Safety behaviour	New alternative behaviour
Avoid particular objects or places.	Gradually expose self to certain objects and places.
Avoid certain forms of transport.	Gradually approach transport. For example, enter stationary train. Get on and off. Work your way towards making a very small trip.
Take specific routes to avoid certain things such as bridges or motorways.	Change route to approach feared things. For example, make a short journey on a quiet motorway, or travel across a small bridge.
Avoid certain tastes, smells, sensations, feelings that might produce anxiety.	Gradually learn to tolerate certain physical or sensory experiences.
Ask for reassurance or others to check things for you.	Avoid asking for reassurance and if you need to check do it yourself.
Avoid watching television about certain feared subjects.	Watch programs about certain feared subjects. Make room for your feelings while you do this.
Try to be in control of others. For example, if phobic of travel trying to give advice to the driver about how to drive safely.	Allow others to drive.

Regulatory organisations in the UK

British Association of Cognitive and Behavioural Psychotherapists
Imperial House
Hornby Street
Bury
Lancashire
BL9 5BN
Tel: 0161 705 4304   Fax: 0161 705 4306
Email: babcp@babcp.com

British Association for Counselling & Psychotherapy
BACP House
15 St John's Business Park
Lutterworth
LE17 4HB
Tel 01455 883300

British Psychological Society
St Andrews House
48 Princess Road East
Leicester
LE1 7DR
United Kingdom
Tel: +44 (0)116 254 9568
Fax: +44 (0)116 227 1314
Email: **enquiries@bps.org.uk**

Health & Care Professional Council
Park House
184 Kennington Park Road,
London
SE11 4BU,
0300 500 6184

Glossary of terms

Abdominal breathing Processing of breathing that involves relaxing the abdomen and taking in air to the bottom of the lungs.

Amygdala Small area of brain tissue within the limbic system, responsible for activating the body's fight-flight-or-freeze response.

Anxiety An emotion that is experienced when the body is moving into a prepared state to deal with a potential threat.

Automatic responses Responses that occur automatically/outside of conscious awareness.

Behavioural strategies Making an adjustment to your behaviour and monitoring the impact of resulting changes.

Catastrophic misinterpretation A frightening and exaggerated thought connected to magnification of perceived stimuli.

Catecholamines Chemical messengers used by cells to communicate with one another.

Cognitive distortions Thinking patterns that distort perception of reality.

Cognitive interventions Strategies based on changing mental reactions.

Cognitive models Ways of explaining how psychological distress is maintained.

Conditioned response A response that occurs automatically as a result of repeated actions towards particular stimuli.

Coping strategies Strategies that have been of some assistance in reducing distress.

Core beliefs Strongly held beliefs about the self.

Counter-intuitive ideas Ideas that we would not naturally gravitate towards.

Default response An automatic response based on previous experiences and past conditioning.

Desensitising Gradually being able to tolerate a feeling by staying in a situation until the feeling feels more bearable.

Diazepam A medication often prescribed as a muscle relaxant.

Dissociation A mental and physical state where an individual feels a loss of connection with his or her body.

Distraction A process that individuals use to avoid experiencing painful emotions.

Emotional reference point A mechanism used by babies who look towards caregivers to determine how they might react at an emotional level.

Experiential A process of experiencing through the senses.

External focus Placing one's attention onto one's external environment.

Habitual behaviours Behaviours that we are inclined to do because we have done them so many times before.

Holistic Multiple processes connected together working in parallel.

Hyperventilation A process of rapid shallow breathing where an individual breathes out too much carbon dioxide.

Hypothesis An idea based on scientific theory.

Intrusive thoughts Thoughts that enter awareness uninvited. These thoughts are usually accompanied by heightened emotion.

Mindfulness A process of staying in the present moment, bringing conscious awareness back to the present, and deliberately moving away from thoughts about the past or the future.

Mood regulation An ability to have some management of one's feelings.

Negative automatic thoughts Thoughts in the background of the mind that have the potential to keep individuals emotionally distressed.

Negative reinforcement A process of repeated behaviour in which negative emotion is reduced, leading to greater likelihood of the same future behaviour.

Neo-cortex Highly developed area of the mind responsible for logical, rational and analytical thinking.

Phobic response An automatic response associated with heightened anxiety, connected to a specific trigger or cue.

Plasticity The brain's ability to repair itself and grow the more that it is used.

Pre-frontal cortex An area of the brain that acts as a relay between the sub-cortical regions of the brain and the neo-cortex. It is also responsible for dampening emotional reactions and quietening the mind.

Registered therapists Registered therapists are members of professional bodies. Professional bodies are organisations that check out their therapists to make sure that they have the required training to do their jobs properly.

Rumination A cognitive process that involves churning of thoughts connected to the self in the past over and over in the mind.

Safety behaviours Behaviours utilised to reduce emotional distress in the short term.

Self-fulfilling prophecy When something occurs despite your very best attempts to prevent that particular thing occurring.

Self-perpetuating A situation that is kept in place through its own actions.

Serotonin A chemical messenger, serotonin plays a huge part in the body's overall physical and mental functioning.

Sub-cortical regions Brain areas located in the lower half of the brain.

Suppressing emotions An act of pushing down painful or upsetting feelings.

Threat perception centre An area within the brain responsible for noticing stimuli associated with past fear or trauma.

Traumatic incidents Events that have occurred in the past connected to highly distressing emotions.

Unprocessed memory An experience that the mind has not fully dealt with.

Vicarious trauma When people develop trauma responses as a result of observing other people's intense emotional reactions.

References and additional reading

Arnsten, A., Raskind, M., Taylor, F. & Connor, D. (2015) The effects of stress exposure on prefrontal cortex: Translating basic research into successful treatments for post-traumatic stress disorder. *Neurobiology of Stress,* pp. 89–99.

Bandura, A. (1977) *Social Learning Theory.* Prentice-Hall.

Beck, J. (2011) *Cognitive Behavior Therapy: Second Edition – Basics and Beyond.* The Guildford Press.

Butler, G. (2009) *Overcoming Social Anxiety & Shyness.* Robinson.

Cabral, R. & Nardi E. (2012) Anxiety and inhibition of panic attacks within translational and prospective research contexts. *Trends in Psychiatry.*

Clark, D.M. (1986) A cognitive approach to panic. *Behaviour Research and Therapy,* 24: 461–470.

Clark, D.M. & Wells, A. (1995) A cognitive model of social phobia. In *Social Phobia – Diagnosis, Assessment, and Treatment* (eds. R.G. Heimberg, M.R. Liebowitz, D. Hope et al.), pp. 69–93. New York: Guilford.

Debiec, J. & Sullivan, R. (2014) Intergenerational transmission of emotional trauma through amygdala-dependent mother-to-infant transfer of specific fear. *Proceedings of the National Academy of Sciences,* DOI: 10.1073/pnas.1316740111

Golman, D. (1996) *Emotional Intelligence: Why It Can Matter More Than IQ.* Bloomsbury.

Greenberger, D. & Padesky, C. (1995) *Mind Over Mood: Change How You Feel by Changing the Way That You Think.* Guildford Press.

Guzmán, Y., Tronson, N., Jovasevic, K., Sato, K., Guedea, A., Mizukami, H., Nishimori, K. & Radulovic. J. (2013) Fear-enhancing effects of septal oxytocin receptors. *Nature Neuroscience,* DOI: 10.1038/nn.3465.

Kennerley, H. (2009) *Overcoming Anxiety: A Self-Help Guide Using Cognitive Behavioural Techniques.* Robinson.

Kinman, G. & Grant, L. (2010) Exploring stress resilience in trainee social workers: The role of emotional and social competencies. *British Journal of Social Work,* 10.1093/bjsw/bcq088.

Krusemark, E. & Li, W. (2012) Enhanced olfactory sensory perception of threat in anxiety: An event-related fMRI study. *Chemosensory Perception,* 5(1): 37 DOI: 10.1007/s12078-011-9111-7.

LeDoux, J.E., Iwata, J., Cicchetti, P., Reis, D.J. (1988) Different projections of the central amygdaloid nucleus mediate autonomic and behavioral correlates of conditioned fear. *Journal of Neuroscience*, Jul;8(7): 2517–29.

Logue, M.W., Bauver, S.R., Kremen, W.S., Franz, C.E., Eisen, S.A., Tsuang, M.T., Grant, M.D. & Lyons, M.J. (2011) Evidence of overlapping genetic diathesis of panic attacks and gastrointestinal disorders in a sample of male twin pairs. *Twin Research and Human Genetics*, Feb; 14(1): 16–24. doi: 10.1375/twin.14.1.16.

McIlrath, D. & Huitt, W. The teaching-learning process: A discussion of models. *Educational Psychology Interactive*. Valdosta, GA: Valdosta State University. Retrieved 2016 from http://www.edpsycinteractive.org/papers/modeltch.html.

Moorey, S. (2010) The six cycles maintenance model: Growing a 'vicious flower' for depression. *Behaviour and Cognitive Psychotherapy*, Mar; 38(2): 173–84.

Moulding, R., Coles, M.E., Abramowitz, J.S., Alcolado, G.M., Alonso, P., Belloch, A., Bouvard, M., Clark, D.A., Doron, G., Fernández-Álvarez, H., García-Soriano, G., Ghisi, M., Gómez, B., Inozu, M., Radomsky, A.S., Shams, G., Sica, C., Simos, G. & Wong, W. (2014) Part 2. They scare because we care: the relationship between obsessive intrusive thoughts and appraisals and control strategies across 15 cities. *Journal of Obsessive-Compulsive and Related Disorders*, 3(3): 280–291.

Rachman, S., Coughtrey, S.R. & Radomsky, A. (2015) *The Oxford Guide to the Treatment of Mental Contamination*. The Oxford University Press.

Seger, C.A. (2011) A critical review of habit learning and the basal ganglia. *Frontiers in Systems Neuroscience*, Aug 30; 5:66.

Teachman, B., Marker, C. & Clerkin, E. (2010) Catastrophic misinterpretations as a predictor of symptom change during treatment for panic disorder. *Journal of Consulting and Clinical Psychology*, 78(6): 964–973.

Veale, D. & Wilson, R. (2005) *Overcoming Obsessive Compulsive Disorder: A Self-help Guide using Cognitive Behavioral Techniques*. Constable & Robinson Ltd.

Wells, A. (1997) *Cognitive Therapy of Anxiety Disorders: A Practice Manual and Conceptual Guide*. Wiley.

Wilson, R. & Veale, D. (2009) *Overcoming Health Anxiety*. Robinson.

Medications commonly prescribed for anxiety disorders or for anxiety disorders with co-morbid depression

Alprazolam A benzodiazepine prescribed for panic, generalised anxiety, phobias, social anxiety and OCD.

Amitriptyline A tricyclic antidepressant.

Atenolol A beta blocker prescribed for anxiety.

Buspirone A mild tranquilliser prescribed for generalised anxiety, OCD and panic.

Chlordiazepoxide A benzodiazepine prescribed for generalised anxiety and phobias.

Citalopram A selective serotonin reuptake inhibitor commonly prescribed for mixed anxiety and depression.

Clomipramine A tricyclic antidepressant.

Clonazepam A benzodiazepine prescribed for panic, generalised anxiety, phobias and social anxiety.

Desipramine A tricyclic antidepressant.

Diazepam A benzodiazepine prescribed for generalised anxiety, panic and phobias.

Doxepin A tricyclic antidepressant.

Duloxetine A serotonin-norepinephrine reuptake inhibitor.

Escitalopram oxalate A selective serotonin reuptake inhibitor.

Fluoxetine A selective serotonin reuptake inhibitor.

Fluvoxamine A selective serotonin reuptake inhibitor.

Gabapentin An anticonvulsant prescribed for generalised anxiety and social anxiety.

Imipramine A tricyclic antidepressant.

Lorazepam A benzodiazepine prescribed for generalised anxiety, panic and phobias.

Nortriptyline A tricyclic antidepressant.

Oxazepam A benzodiazepine prescribed for generalised anxiety and phobias.

Paroxetine A selective serotonin reuptake inhibitor.

Phenelzine A monoamine oxidase inhibitor.

Pregabalin An anticonvulsant prescribed for generalised anxiety disorder.

Propanalol A beta blocker prescribed for anxiety.

Sertraline A selective serotonin reuptake inhibitor.

Tranylcypromine A monoamine oxidase inhibitor.

Valproate An anticonvulsant prescribed for panic.

Venlafaxine A serotonin-norepinephrine reuptake inhibitor.

Made in the USA
Middletown, DE
11 January 2021